WORKING

YOUR

FINANCIAL

DESTINY

DR. CHIBUNDO ANENE

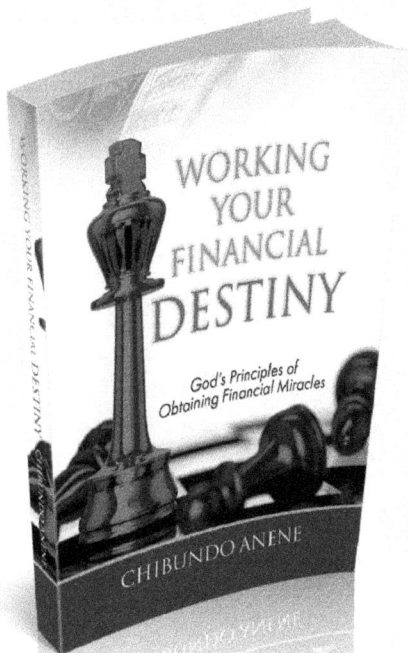

WORKING YOUR FINANCIAL DESTINY

God's Principles of Obtaining Financial Miracles

CHIBUNDO ANENE

REHOBOTH HOUSETM

WORKING YOUR FINANCIAL DESTINY

Copyright © 2019 By Dr. Chibundo Anene

ISBN: 978-1-64301-018-2

Bible references are taken from the King James Version of the Bible unless otherwise stated.

Forward enquiries to Dr. Chibundo Anene for counseling, teachings, seminars, and workshops.

Author's Contact: *chibundoanene@yahoo.com*
Or call 01-804-502-1926

Interior and Cover Designed by Rehoboth House, Chicago
www.rehobothhouseonline.com
email:info@rehobothhouseonline.com

Printed in United States of America

REHOBOTH HOUSE

Table Of Contents

ACKNOWLEDGMENT

I appreciate my father, pastor and mentor; Pastor Toye Ademola who has received a mandate of prosperity from our Lord, making everyone who listens to him prosper. My life has been significantly challenged and transformed by his life and messages.

Thank you Pastor Wumi for your exemplary motherhood and leadership. You with Pastor Toye are making many great. Love you, Mom.

I appreciate the entire DIC/CTMI Pastoral team and family. You are an amazing great team.

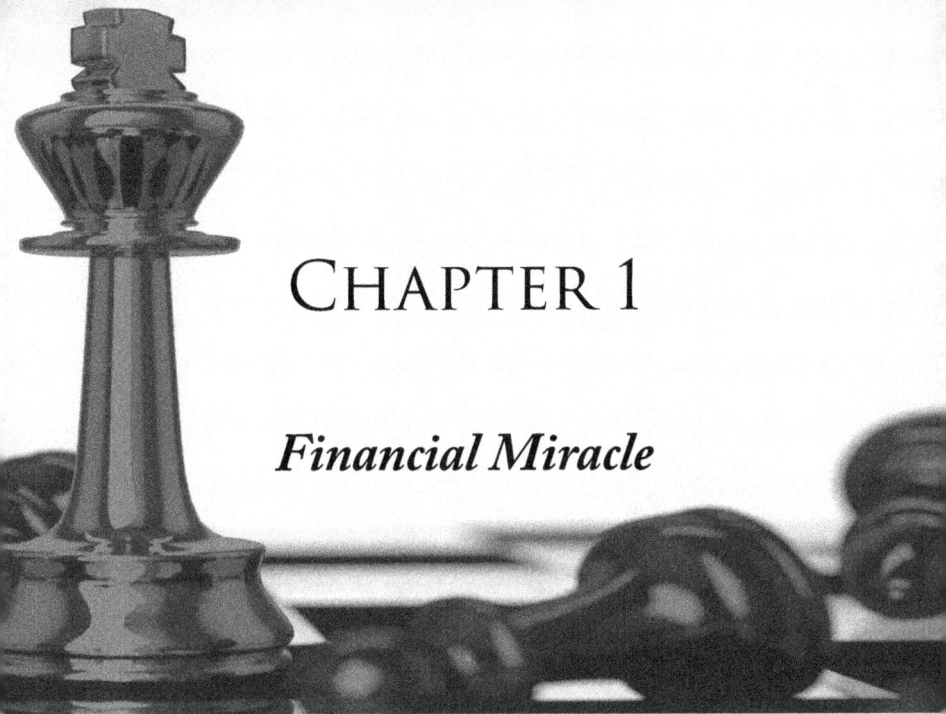

CHAPTER 1

Financial Miracle

Your belief in financial miracle is a prerequisite to reading this book. For you to experience the kind of financial destiny God has for you, you must believe in financial miracles. By this, I mean God supernaturally providing finances abundantly. I do not think it is a hard thing for God to release finances supernaturally if He raised Jesus from death. God can heal, restore, and intervene miraculously. God is a God of miracles, and we have experienced His miracle in various ways. But I tell you, your experience of God's miracles would not be complete without financial miracle because all things answer to money.

> *"A feast is made for laughter, and wine maketh merry: but money answereth all things." (Eccl 10:19)*

You must experience a financial miracle to be in dominion; to live a fulfilled life after God's purpose. It doesn't matter how highly anointed you are, you need money, or your anointing will lead to frustration. Anointing has its place and money has its own place in ministry. Anointing can never take the place of money or vice versa.

In fact, the anointing that is incapable of producing money is questionable *"... for it is he that giveth thee power to get wealth..."* (Deut. 8:18). When God anoints you with His power, one of the by-products is money to prosper His will. This is why this book is a must-read for anyone one that wants to excel in God's purpose. I am excited that God has made provision for every of His child to prosper beyond every limitation, economic situation, background, job market, etc.

What Is A Financial Miracle?

I will simply define a financial miracle as having income beyond and above your means (jobs), circumstance and expectations; God supplying you finances above and beyond what you can ask, think, imagine or dream.

> *"Now to Him who is able to do exceedingly abundantly above all that we ask or think, according to the power that works in us"* (Eph. 3:20).

Financial miracle is possible because God is able. Jesus came to preach to the poor so that they might become rich through the word.

> *"The blind receive their sight, and the lame walk, the lepers are cleansed, and the deaf hears, the dead are raised up, and the poor have the gospel preached to them." (Mt. 11:5)*

> *"As sorrowful, yet always rejoicing; as poor, yet making many rich; as having nothing, and yet possessing all things" (2 Cor. 6: 10).*

And the same commission He has committed to me. I want to declare that I am sent to make you rich through this book. You that have limited income will break forth on the left and right, and abound in all things. Get set for an overflow.

> *"Enlarge the place of your tent, And let them stretch out the curtains of your dwellings; Do not spare; Lengthen your cords, And strengthen your stakes. (Is. 54:2)*

When you receive the word of Christ through this book, the spirit of Christ will invade your life and circumstance and cause a financial miracle.

> *"And you shall remember the Lord your God, for it is He who*

gives you the power to get wealth, that He may establish His covenant which He swore to your fathers, as it is this day" (Deut. 8:18).

You that are limited financially get set for abundance.

How Do I Get Set?

When Peter made his mind up to give up his expertise and wisdom and try the word that seemed foolish, he encountered a turnaround in his business and finance. (Luke 5: 4-7). Mary, the mother of Jesus, told the disciple's

"Whatever he asks you to do, do it" (John 2: 5).

Who amongst you will believe and obey God's principles in this book, to such will the Lord's arm shall be revealed for abundance. Get set your time for a financial miracle is now by your deliberate choice to believe and obey God's principles as contained in this book.

If that is your choice, I say congratulations to you in advance because your financial destiny is here and sure. And also I commend you to God and the word of this grace which is able to build you up and give you an inheritance amongst them that are sanctified.

Amplified Version Puts It This Way

"And now brethren I commit you to God. And I commend you to the word of His grace (to the Command and Counsels and

Promises of His unmerited favour, it is able to build you up and to give your (your rightful) inheritance among all God's set apart ones (those consecrated, purified and transformed of God)" (Acts 20:32).

There is an inheritance even financial destiny prepared for you, but you have to be built up to acquire it. The word primarily has a work of building you up before you can obtain your financial destiny. Therefore you must take God's word as a command (non-negotiable), counsel (wisdom from God).

When you see the principles revealed in this book as a command and counsel, you have no choice than to obey. If you must arrive at your financial destiny, what you feel or know should not count. You must choose to obey the word of God against your will; this is <u>working</u> on your financial destiny. Obeying God's word especially when it is against your will is work, hence the book title; Working Your Financial Destiny. When you work the word, the word works for you the miracle you desire.

Working financial destiny simply means working God's word (principles) on finances that in turn delivers your financial destiny, giving you the financial miracle you desire. What the Lord lays in my heart to share with you is this book worked in Bible days and still works today.

It worked for the Zarephath widow; she obeyed the word and realized her financial destiny in 1 Kings 17. The Prophet's widow obeyed God's word from Elisha and entered hers.

Peter obeyed Jesus' word and experienced a financial miracle in Mt 17: 24 -27. The list is endless. And space would fail me to list men and women of today's world who have entered their financial destiny.

One common factor amongst all those who realized their financial destiny is simple obedience to the word of God. I tell you financial destiny is real and available so put your name on the list by your resolved commitment to the word.

Who Needs Financial Miracle?

Everyone needs it, especially the financially poor. The poor are people limited in their income. Through this book, command and counsel from God's word will be coming to you like it did for the above beneficiaries, only resolve to obey in spite of the odds, lack, and limitations. Some words will come as commands I beg of you to obey unconditionally, even if they contradict your belief and knowledge.

> *"Wherefore lay apart all filthiness and superfluity of naughtiness, and receive with meekness the engrafted word, which is able to save your souls" (James 1:21).*

Amplified puts it this way:

> *"So get rid of all uncleanness and the rampant outgrowth of wickedness, and in a humble (gentle, modest) spirit receive and welcome the word which implanted and rooted (in your hearts) contains the <u>power</u> (spirit) to save your souls."*

When you accept the word and obey, your soul, by the spirit, is empowered over poverty and saved from poverty. If what you have known this long while has been unable to change your financial state, why not try God's knowledge; wisdom and word. Let your heart be opened to new ideas and ways that are in line with God's word.

> *"Receive, I pray you, the law and instruction from His mouth (God's mouth) and lay up His word in your heart. If you return to the Almighty (and submit and humble yourself before Him), you will be built up, if you put away unrighteousness far from your tents. If you lay gold on the dust, and the gold of Ophir among the stones of the brook (considering them of little worth) yea the Almighty shall be thy defence and thou shalt have plenty of silver. Then you will have delight in the Almighty, and you will lift up your face to God. You will make your prayer to Him, and He will hear you, and you will pay your vow. And you shall also decide and decree a thing, and it shall be established for you and the light (of God's favour) shalt shine upon your ways. When men are cast down, then thou shalt say, there is lifting up, and he shall save the humble person. He will even deliver the one (For whom you intercede) who is not innocent, yes he will be delivered through the cleanness of your hands" (Job 22: 22-30).*

I would like to say here that the vehicle for a financial miracle is God's word and nothing else. The power that is in what God says is that power (spirit) that makes wealth, and this power is released through your obedience to God's word to you.

> *"Riches and honour are with me, yea durable riches and unrighteousness." (Prov. 8:18)*

> *"Exalt her, and she shall promote thee; she shall bring thee to honour when thou dost embrace her. She shall give to thine head an ornament of grace; a crown of glory shall she deliver to thee" (Prov. 4: 8-9).*

> *"If you listen diligently to the voice of the Lord your God, being watchful to do all His commandment (word) which I command you this day, the Lord your God will set you high above the earth. And all these blessings shall come upon you and overtake you if you heed the voice of the Lord your God" (Deut. 28: 1-2).*

The word of God is the only tool or vehicle to your financial destiny, so esteem it highly. Take heed to the principles coming to you from this book, lay them up in your heart and obey. If financial destiny is your desire, be set to trade your wisdom and knowledge for His word, command, and counsel. (1Cor 3:18-19)

Before I conclude this chapter, I'd love to define financial destiny as financial provision God has made available to you; in other words, God's expectation and desire for your finance.

> *"Beloved, I wish above all things that thou mayest prosper and be in health, even as thy soul prospereth" (3 John 1: 2).*

God expects you to increase and abound. Financial destiny is a state you abound in all things lacking nothing.

> *"And Abraham was old, and well stricken in age: and the LORD had blessed Abraham in all things" (Gen. 24:1).*

A state where you are increased and comforted on every side; where you have all sufficiency in all things, and abound to every good work.

A place where money is no more the determining factor because you have the means and ability to do that which is in your heart.

These Describe Financial Destiny

> *Good news, "God is able to make all grace abound towards you, that ye, always having all sufficiency in all things may abound to every good work" (2 Cor. 9:8).*

It may seem impossible, but with God, all things are possible. The only thing that can take you to your financial destiny is a financial miracle, God supernaturally supplying beyond your means and ability. To realize your financial destiny, financial miracle is a must.

God releases grace to you for financial miracle through His word. Embrace His word wholeheartedly, and the grace in the word will cause a financial release on you. From creation, God demonstrated His desire for your financial destiny. He made everything abundant for Adam in the Garden of Eden.

Today, by the death and resurrection of Jesus He has provided a new and living way for you back to Garden of Eden, only trace it by His word. Taking steps by the word, you will surely arrive at your financial destiny.

CHAPTER 2

Fundamentals of Financial Miracle

In the previous chapter of the book, I emphasised that financial miracle is a must for financial destiny because your means or ability cannot take you to the state of abounding in all things and lacking nothing. Therefore there are basic things you should know and understand about financial miracle; fundamentals of financial miracle.

This knowledge must be in place before you can experience your financial miracle as intended by God.

God's Word Is The Conveyor Of Financial Miracle

- Prov. 3:18-21
- Prov. 3:13-14
- Acts 20:32
- Prov. 13:18

If financial destiny is your desire, take the word of God as a commandment, not a suggestion; and be willing to obey unconditionally.

> *"Therefore, holy brethren, partakers of the heavenly calling, consider the Apostle and High Priest of our confession, Christ Jesus, who was faithful to Him who appointed Him, as Moses also was faithful in all His house. For this One has been counted worthy of more glory than Moses, inasmuch as He who built the house has more honor than the house" (Heb. 3: 1-3 NKJV).*

Search the word as you would precious gold. Labour in the word and you will not labour for money

Have Absolute Faith In The Servant Of God Declaring God's Word To You

God's servant is God's mouthpiece (Oracle) that declares God's word that ushers your increase and abundance. Before God does a miracle, He must need to send His servants to speak the word.

> *"For whosoever shall call upon the name of the Lord shall be saved. How then shall they call on him in whom they have*

> *not believed? And how shall they believe in him of whom they have not heard? And how shall they hear without a preacher? And how shall they preach, except they be sent? As it is written, How beautiful are the feet of them that preach the gospel of peace, and bring glad tidings of good things! But they have not all obeyed the gospel. For Esaias saith, Lord, who hath believed our report?" (Rom. 10:13-16).*

> *"Who hath believed our report? And to whom is the arm of the LORD revealed?" (Is. 53:1).*

Your choice to believe the servant of God is to your advantage and not a favour to him. Whether you believe him or not, he is called of God. Your vote is needless to validate his calling. I know I am called and highly anointed to write this book for you, your choice to believe what I have written is for your good and does not add or subtract from my calling and commission. It is funny for people to think that their belief on a servant of God is to make him feel good.

I once had a member that calls when she feels good and says "Apostle Chi" I believe you are a "woman of God" and on other occasions, she doubts my calling. Little did she know her believing in me is for her good and not mine, because God does not need her vote or counsel to keep me in ministry. And not too long, she left the ministry and could not prosper in God's will for herself because of her lack of confidence in me.

> *Do you want to prosper in God's will for your life? It is very important you believe God's servant to you. "And they rose early in the morning, and went forth into the wilderness of Tekoa: and as they went forth, Jehoshaphat stood and said, Hear me, O Judah, and ye inhabitants of Jerusalem; Believe in the LORD your God, so shall ye be established; believe his prophets, so shall ye prosper" (2 Chron. 20:20).*

While this lady doubted, many that believed were having testimonies of God's faithfulness. God's servants are God's messenger and gift for your good; you will do yourself well to believe in them. Your belief should be demonstrated in obeying what they say. When you believe and obey the word the servant of God speaks, you are rewarded with the blessings of the word (prophet's reward).

I am only a messenger. The word or principles I share in this book are not mine or my ideas. Nor do I write what I am able to do but what He is set and able to do in your life. So look beyond my ability or stature and believe God's magnanimous ability. It does not matter your financial state today only obey my voice (God's word) as revealed in this book, you shall be lifted.

> *"Who is among you that feareth the LORD, that obeyeth the voice of his servant, that walketh in darkness, and hath no light? let him trust in the name of the LORD, and stay upon his God" (Is. 50:10).*

God whose word I write can raise a beggar from a dunghill to dine with princes. The easiest way the devil can cut you off from your financial destiny is to make you doubt the authenticity of the principles contained in this book, refuse it. This book in your hands is inspired by God and sent your way to help you change your financial status, so choose to believe it.

Change Your View About Money And Possession

Money is a tool, your messenger, and not your Lord and master. So be ready and willing to let go of it and send it on an errand to get what you need. A wise man once said, "If what's in your hand is not enough for what you need. Sow it for the harvest for your need." I have tried it, and it works.

Be willing to sow for the harvest of your financial desire and destiny. The reason many are not blessed financially is due to the reluctance to sow money. What you sow you reap. If you sow money, you reap money.

> *"Be not deceived; God is not mocked: for whatsoever a man soweth, that shall he also reap" (Gal. 6: 7).*

This is the principle of life and increase. Majority of Christians would render any service, but when it comes to money, it is a different issue. Anything you cannot give owns you and is your Lord. I am sorry to say this, if you are not willing to give your money, money owns you and is your lord. You are its slave and not the owner. Today I break you from every form of slavery to money as I release the spirit of giving on you.

When you cannot part with money, it shows you are in love with money, which the Bible says is the beginning (root) of all evil.

> *"For the love of money is a root of all kinds of evil, for which some have strayed from the faith in their greediness, and pierced themselves through with many sorrows" (1 Tim. 6:10).*

I have something to tell you, note very well: the money you presently have is a test if you will sow it for the true riches (financial destiny). The money you have now is a seed God has given you for your financial destiny. So keep sowing till you arrive at your financial destiny. If you stop sowing you stop having. Consider all the money in your possession a potential seed. So be excited to sow.

Learn To Give

It is sad that many cannot spend on themselves leave alone giving. Such persons believe all that the preacher is preaching except the subject of giving. When he teaches giving to God's work, they murmur; "this preacher has come again, thieves, can't he preach something else." By this attitude, he disconnects from his financial blessing.

He does these because of his wrong view and mentality about money.

Many had left the ministry when we ran this series on financial destiny because of giving. One of them called me and said, "Dr. Chi if you are preaching tithing and giving money I will stop coming," and indeed she stopped. I wish I could make her stay. But I have not found an alternative way to financial destiny in the Bible than through giving.

For this reason, I shall be discussing an important topic "Learning to Give" in the next chapter.

No one man is born with the nature to give, giving is not a trait, it is learnt. If you are in the above category, please, do not close this book, you can learn to give, so you will willingly apply the principles in this book. Do not quit like the ones that left the ministry and did not complete the series.

I want you to be a giver so that you will arrive at the financial destiny God has prepared for you. Anything that will hinder you from giving keeps you perpetually bound to poverty. I rebuke it in the mighty name of Jesus. Do not let your love for money deprive you of your financial inheritance. When you love money so much not to give, you will look for alternative ways to get I, and this leads to evil.

People that do not give to increase God's way hoard, steal, sell their bodies, kill, etc. And these are evil.

"For the love of money is the root of all evil" (1 Tim 6:10).

The love for money prevents you from sowing to harvest. When you love money, you cannot lay it as dust for your harvest, like the early Church did in Acts of Apostles.

"Receive, I pray thee, the law from his mouth, and lay up his words in thine heart. If thou return to the Almighty, thou shalt be built up, thou shalt put away iniquity far from thy tabernacles" (Job 22:22-23).

To lay gold as dust is to put it in its right place as a tool or messenger; willing and ready to sow it. In the world and kingdom, the people that prosper financially are people that have little or no regards for money.

"He that scatters have more than enough…" (Prov. 11:24).

There is a glorious financial destiny for you in Christ. Do not exchange it for the peanuts in your hands by your reluctance to sow (give). It is a pity when someone believes all that God says in every area except in giving. It is the devil's ploy to keep you poor. If you cannot give God your money, it shows you love your money more than God, and you are living a limited lifestyle. Until you give God your money, you cannot have the money God has kept for you.

All Money Belongs To God: Hag 2:8, Ps 24:1, Jn3:27

Everything here on earth is God's, even the money in your pocket and bank account. If they are God's, why behave like you did not receive it by your unwillingness to give it back to Him. Your attitude should be "If God, the owner needs it, I will give it to him than keep it." If you keep back money when the owner demands it, you become an illegitimate holder; a thief and cursed. With this understanding, I willingly and excitedly give when He demands it or whenever I sense a need in the kingdom.

Do not be like the rich man in Luke 12 that was not rich towards God. He did not give to God. No wonder the Bible called him a fool.

He was foolish not to recognize that his ground was fruitful because of God, and the ground was God's, because of his foolishness, he was cursed. Anything that makes you keep back from God is not wisdom, but stupidity, and setting you up for curse. Any money you cannot give to God you will lose to curse of sickness, accident, etc. Be wise.

You either give to the owner or lose it to the devil through curses. Your financial blessing and sustenance is from God and not your job.

The reason you work is to keep busy, invest your time and talent, and be a blessing to others.

Your Blessings Come From God

> *"I will lift up mine eyes unto the hills, from whence cometh my help. My help cometh from the LORD, which made heaven and earth" (Ps 121: 1-2).*

It is essential you know this truth so that you will not be limited in your faith and expect more from God than your income. Until you know this God would not provide for you beyond your salary.

> *"Let it be done to you according to your faith" (Matt 9:29).*

Some have limited their faith to their job and cannot receive from God beyond their salary.

How do I know? They plan and budget only within their salary. My oldest sister, Chiko, believes and lives this fact that God is her supplier, by her regular paying of tithes, offerings, and kingdom projects. Most times, she gives beyond her means. And God has proved He is her sustenance by miraculously providing for her. Recently God stirred the heart of someone to sponsor her holiday trip to the USA, which could not have been possible based on her income.

When you hold on tightly to your salary and not willing to give, you depend on it, and God is handicapped to bless you beyond your income.

Many Christians today profess faith in God, but in reality, their faith is on their salary. I want you to deliberately remove eyes from the hill (your salary) and look up to Him for your sustenance. When you have done this, you will go full length in giving for your financial destiny. What if God demands you to give your total salary (Isaac) will you be willing to? Be ready to enlarge your coast beyond your job by giving generously.

> *"And I will shake all nations, and the desire of all nations shall come: and I will fill this house with glory, saith the LORD of hosts. The silver is mine, and the gold is mine, saith the LORD of hosts" (Hag. 2:7-8).*

God shakes heaven and earth and everywhere to release gold and silver to you. Heaven and earth etc. are definitely beyond your job, company or business, so be ready to go beyond your job. Make budgets and plans beyond your income and see God fulfil it. Let your dream not be limited. Remove your faith from your job and believe God for more avenues for your financial blessing.

The reason you are not blessed beyond where you are now is that you have limited God to provide you only through your job. Many have committed suicide because they lost their job or could not get a job. God is above that; do not limit Him in your thoughts and ways.

> *"Therefore I tell you, do not worry about your life, what you will eat or drink; or about your body, what you will wear. Is not life more than food, and the body more than clothes? Look at the birds of the air; they do not sow or reap or store away in barns, and yet your heavenly Father feeds them. Are you not much more valuable than they? Can any one of you by worrying add a single hour to your life? "And why do you worry about clothes? See how the flowers of the field grow. They do not labor or spin. 29 Yet I tell you that not even Solomon in all his splendor was dressed like one of these. 30 If that is how God clothes the grass of the field, which is here today and tomorrow is thrown into the fire, will he not much more clothe you—you of little faith? 31 So do not worry, saying, 'What shall we eat?' or 'What shall we drink?' or 'What shall we wear?' (Mt 6: 25-31).*

When you calculate and budget around your income and cannot give, it shows you have faith in your job, not in God. I am not saying you should live above your present means for that is covetousness and greed. What I am saying is make plans outside your income, enlarge your mind and sow part of your income as a seed for God to meet your budget. When the dream is in your heart, God will put it in your hands. You must see it first to possess it. Your job is the means which you get the seed to sow for your financial desire.

"And God blessed them, and God said unto them, Be fruitful, and multiply, and replenish the earth, and subdue it: and have dominion over the fish of the sea, and over the fowl of the air, and over every living thing that moveth upon the earth. And God said, Behold, I have given you every herb bearing seed, which is upon the face of all the earth, and every tree, in the which is the fruit of a tree yielding seed; to you, it shall be for meat" (Gen 1:28-29).

Financial Miracle Is For The Poor

Jesus came to preach to the poor and was made poor so that the poor through the poverty of Jesus they might be made rich. Who is poor? Anyone limited in his means, when what you have is not enough to meet your needs. So do not count yourself out. You that are limited in your means should be willing to operate the principle of financial destiny, particularly the principle of giving. When it is time to give, do not count yourself out and expect only the rich to give. If there is anyone that should give for multiplication of resources, it is you that are limited. In fact, when the Pastor is asking for people to give it is you, he has been sent to for your abundance.

Most often, people shift the privilege to give to someone else and have consequently missed out of God's blessing. Giving is actually for the poor so they too can harvest. That is why Jesus came to preach to them so that through their obedience, they might be rich. No matter how poor you are, you have something to give. Be set to give as the Spirit ministers to you.

David Youngi Cho told of a poor lady that gave the only pot she had for their church building, and that established her in the financial destiny. Be set to release that which you have for your financial destiny. Give yourself to greatness. If you do not like your financial state, give your way into your financial destiny.

• Giving is the steps in the ladder of financial destiny.

• Giving remains an eternal solution to financial crisis, not praying and fasting.

"And if ye do good to them which do good to you, what thank have ye? for sinners also do even the same." (Luke 6:33).

"Be not deceived; God is not mocked: for whatsoever a man soweth, that shall he also reap" (Gal. 6:7).

If it means giving your last and all like the widow of Zarephath, do it, but do not remain in that financial state.

Sowing for financial destiny does not only mean money but anything that can be exchanged for money. Cash or kind in the secular term.

In one of our services, a woman during the offering gave her a golden necklace for the church project. Some have given clothes, houses, cars, furniture, etc. This option offers you the opportunity not to be left out. If you are giving in-kind give something worthwhile that can be traded if need be. It is scriptural.

Your seed may leave your hand but definitely not your life.

> *"Cast thy bread upon the waters: for thou shalt find it after many days" (Eccl. 11:1).*

> *"Now he that ministereth seed to the sower both minister bread for your food, and multiply your seed sown, and increase the fruits of your righteousness" (2 Cor. 9:10).*

> *"While the earth remaineth, seedtime and harvest, and cold and heat, and summer and winter, and day and night shall not cease" (Gen 8:22).*

When God demands your money, it is so that He can multiply it for your harvest. He accepts your seed, multiplies it, and returns it into your life. Seed sowing is the principle of life that guarantees increase in every area.

Giving Is Not A Gift, It Is Learned

People that give learnt it, so do not expect to love it or feel like it when you start giving. No one does, people grow themselves into that. It is never comfortable with anyone at the beginning.

> *"He that goeth forth and weepeth, bearing precious seed, shall doubtless come again with rejoicing, bringing his sheaves with him" (Ps. 126:6).*

So learn to give, be patient in giving and do not quit when you feel the pinch and pain. There is no seed sowing without weeping and tears; only consider the price ahead and bear it. Giving is not one of the spiritual gifts.

In this book, I shall be teaching you how to give. I was taught, and now, it is my turn to teach you. After I learnt, giving ceased to be a concern. I will ever remain grateful to my teachers; it was not easy at first, but today, I am grateful for the liberty I enjoy.

Until you give liberally, you are not liberated. Man's nature is selfish; just about himself. Until you learn to give, you are not released from self. Today there is nothing God will ask me to give that I will not give gladly.

Giving Is Sacrificial

No one has it all. Every time you give, you are letting go of a need or demand. So be ready to let go of a need to give and meet a need in God's kingdom. Have a scale of preference do some opportunity cost that favours kingdom needs. In your scale of preference, let God's kingdom need be your priority in your giving, and give it cheerfully.

I remembered in 2001, I saved some money to buy an outfit and accessories for the memorial service of my late mum. I went to church and the pastor announced the need for an amplifier and mixer, whose price was just the amount I had saved. Without a second thought, I quickly gave the money to get the amplifier and mixer.

The kingdom is my priority. I cannot imagine wearing a new dress while the church's need is not met yet. Until Christ returns, the kingdom remains my priority before anything or anyone else. Everyone in my family shares the same view. Each time we make Him our priority, He turns around and meets our needs abundantly.

And guess what, God made someone get me the dress and shoe even better than I could afford. When you let go of a need to meet His, He turns around and meets your need even in a much better way. I encourage you to make the kingdom your priority.

The reason you cannot give to kingdom work yet is that it is the last on your list or not there at all. You will claim "I do not have" but you go about eating and drinking, changing clothes, etc. You do not pay your bill because you have the money; you pay your bills because it makes amenities available to you. Same way, giving to God kingdom makes heaven resource abound towards you.

Giving Is Not A Debt You Owe But A Seed You Sow

You must not give to God with the attitude of payback:

you do not owe God. How much can you pay for your salvation or pay for all His blessing in your life? Moreover, the money you give is His. So do not give out of religious obligation, but from a grateful heart.

I consider it a privilege to give to God, who has given me so much. It is not a debt I owe but a love seed I sow.

Make God Your Financial Partner And Adviser

Let Him dictate how you spend your money. If God trusts you, He releases more and takes you to your financial destiny. Though you earned money and it is rightfully yours, let Him decide how best to spend it.

I know a businessman, in fact, my brother-in-law, He lets God decide what to do with his profit, who to help, what to invest in, etc. I made that choice a long time ago even to the last detail.

God will not commit increase to you when you waste resources. Be prudent and **kingdom minded.** When Jesus fed the five thousand, His disciples followed His instruction to the last. How to get the men to sit, how to distribute, and what to do with the remnant? In the same way, God is interested in how you spend your money, this abundance in your hands. Many have bought things God did not approve, even invested outside God's will, and this has hindered their financial destiny.

At the onset of our ministry, God told us, "Be careful not to waste my resources"- we (the leaders) knew what He meant. It means that we should be careful not to invest outside His will. For every financial involvement, we seek His will. There have been instances we had to stop some projects. Lack of financial prudence is the major reason many ministries, businesses, homes, lives have been strangulated. God is able and will supply, but this is phase by phase.

Men are in sizes and life too is in phases. Live and enjoy your financial phase today or tomorrow will be elusive. If you do not respect your financial phase today, you will not get to your financial destiny tomorrow.

I hope this fundamental has helped you and got you set; giving you the right mind to work your financial destiny. This is a foundation for subsequent chapters and teaching. You have a financial destiny in Christ, and I believe this chapter has got you set.

The foundation of your financial destiny has been laid, come with me, let's start the building.

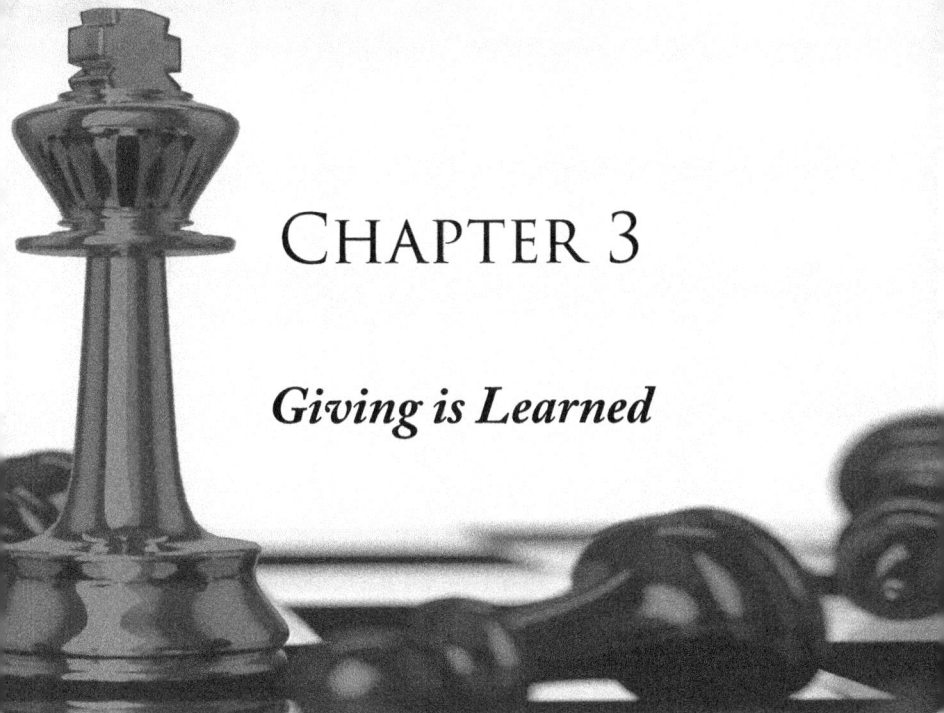

CHAPTER 3

Giving is Learned

This is an essential chapter in this book because the answer to a financial miracle is GIVING. It is my prayer that by the end of this chapter, you will begin to find giving delightsome. As I watch my little baby grow into a boy, I observe he is hesitant to give, even the things I just gave him. One day I had just given him some slices of apple, I asked him for a slice he refused, and when, against his will, I took a bite he became hysteric, threw tantrums, and threw the rest away. I had to calm him down and apologized. To him, I had violated his right. However, he forgot that I gave him the apple in the first place.

I paused and wondered, do we not most times, if not always behave that way to God, the one that gave us all the blessings. Don't we feel we are being violated when God demands something from us? And what God demands is as little as a bite or a slice from the bunch of blessing He has given.

After my experience with my two-year-old toddler, I understood better the relevance of this chapter. If no one taught my baby how not to give, then giving is not natural with men and should be learnt.

I have a few questions I will take you through, and I will be done with this chapter.

- Why learn to give?

- From who and where do I learn to give?

- What did they give?

- What prompted their giving?

- Rewards of their giving?

- Consequences of not giving?

Why Learn To Give?

* Giving is the eternal solution to financial crisis and has no substitute or alternative.

"And if ye do good to them which do good to you, what thank have ye? For sinners also do even the same" (Luke 6:33).

"And God remembered Noah, and every living thing, and all the cattle that was with him in the ark: and God made a wind to pass over the earth, and the waters asswaged" (Gen 8:11).

"There is that scattereth, and yet increaseth, and there is that withholdeth more than is meet, but it tendeth to poverty. The liberal soul shall be made fat: and he that watereth shall be watered also himself. He that withholdeth corn, the people shall curse him: but blessing shall be upon the head of him that selleth it" (Prov.11:24-26).

If financial destiny is your desire, you must learn to give and begin to give. If you desire to prosper financially, then you must start giving. Nothing answers to financial lack than giving.

* Another reason is that giving is not natural. By nature, mankind is selfish; "me and me alone" and wants to amass as much as possible. After the fall of man in Adam, we lost God's nature and character, including the power to give.

"But sin, taking occasion by the commandment, wrought in me all manner of concupiscence. For without the law, sin was dead" (Rom 7: 18).

Do not feel bad when you do not give and do not give up on yourself, only learn.

- The third reason giving is learned is because man does not have a place for God in his heart and would instead give to any other cause than God's kingdom purpose.

This is why someone can spend a considerable amount of money on partying, friends, politics, etc. and would not give a dime to God and His cause. For these and many other reasons giving should be learned.

Who And Where Do I Learn To Give?

Example, they say is the best teacher. Life is the best example. I am a good learner. I observe people and learn from them. So you can learn to give from the lives of committed and habitual givers in the past and present. And the Bible is a good catalogue of lives of givers you can learn from.

> *"Now all these things happened unto them for ensamples: and they are written for our admonition, upon whom the ends of the world are come" (1 Cor. 10: 11).*

When you come in contact with a habitual giver, it is a great opportunity to learn. Let his giving influence you positively rather than condemn or think he is foolish.

A giver is not stupid but wise because giving is God's wisdom for an increase.

"There is that scattereth, and yet increaseth, and there is that withholdeth more than is meet, but it tendeth to poverty. (Prov.11:24).

When you scatter (give), your seed is multiplied and given back to you for increase. This is God's wisdom for increase. If your husband or wife is a giver, do not discourage him or her but learn from him or her for your increase.

As you learn and begin to give, you move from one level of giving to the other, thereby excelling in your financial destiny. There is always the next level of giving for greater height in your financial destiny. A truly fulfilled life is in giving.

"And God said, Behold, I have given you every herb bearing seed, which is upon the face of all the earth, and every tree, in the which is the fruit of a tree yielding seed; to you, it shall be for meat" (Gen 1:29).

Giving is like sowing seed, which releases the power to dominate, replenish, and subdue the earth to you. You have not started living until you are a giver.

We shall be considering some examples of givers, what they gave, and the reward.

God

You cannot talk about givers without mentioning God. First, God is the greatest giver.

> *"For God so loved the world, that he gave his only begotten Son, that whosoever believeth in him should not perish, but have everlasting life" (Jn. 3:16).*

God, from the beginning of creation, is always looking for a way to give to mankind. Giving to people that are not even worthy of His love and gifts. From Genesis to Revelation, God is about giving. From creation to eternity, He is still about giving. He cannot change.

He gave Adam His Spirit, Eve, the Garden of Eden, fowls of the air and other creation– these gifts were all about making Adam comfortable and fulfilled.

> *"How precious also are thy thoughts unto me, O God! how great is the sum of them" (Ps. 139:17).*

> *"Beloved, I wish above all things that thou mayest prosper and be in health, even as thy soul prospereth" (3 Jn. 2).*

God is consumed with ways of giving to you; to add to you. Even when Adam failed, He did not give up on mankind. Rather, He gave man His only begotten son for redemption. And with Him, God gave mankind all things to enjoy. All that Adam lost He gave back to us through Jesus.

"The thief cometh not, but for to steal, and to kill, and to destroy: I have come that they might have life and that they might have it more abundantly"(Jn. 10:10).

Through Jesus, God's gift to you, all things are yours. God gave all things, nothing excluded.

"For all things, are yours" (1 Cor. 3: 21b).

To date, God is still in the business of giving. Right now, God is willing to give you all that you ask. If you need anything, ask, and He will freely (without condition) give it to you.

"For I am persuaded, that neither death, nor life, nor angels, nor principalities, nor powers, nor things present, nor things to come" (Rom. 8: 38).

What a generous giver is our God. He does withhold any good thing from you. The problem is that you do not ask. If you ask, you can be sure to receive.

"Ask, and it will be given to you; seek, and you will find; knock, and it will be opened to you"(Matt. 7:7).

Open your mouth wide, and He will fill it. Pause a moment, what are the things you need or want, they are already yours. That good life you desire is yours. God will not hoard it from you.

"For the LORD, God is a sun and shield: the LORD will give grace and glory: no good thing will he withhold from them that walk uprightly" (Ps. 84:11).

God has given you His son, His spirit, and all you will ever need. God's love is the basis for answered prayer.

Why Does God Give?

He gives because of His love for man. Man's need for salvation. God is about your welfare and interest.

Reward of His Giving

What did God gain from His giving? He harvested many sons. If He did not give, He would have been God by Himself, with no people. Because of His gift, we are now His children (people of God).

"But as many as received him, to them gave he the power to become the sons of God, even to them that believe on his name." (Jn. 1:12)

If God did not give His son, He would have been alone with His son, having one son, but now He has many sons, and He is God over all.

Jesus Gave

Jesus is not only a giver, but He is God's ordained life for our example. Jesus is the eternal example to the heir of salvation. No wonder He said; *"Come and learn of me and find rest to your soul" (Mt. 11:28- 30).*

Surely He has a lot to teach souls in times of financial crisis. If there is anything that bothers people most, it is lack of finances. Jesus has a lot to teach on giving, humbly accept, and find rest to your soul.

> He said; *"Except a grain of corn falls to the ground and dies it abides alone" (Jn. 12:24).*

To emphasise the importance of giving, He likened the kingdom of God to it. That goes to say that giving is a fundamental principle of the kingdom.

About Himself, He said, *"I have power to lay it down and power to take it up."* (Jn. 10:18) Jesus understands the fact that it takes power to give, power to go against the contrary wind that wants to stop you from giving.

> *"He that observeth the wind shall not sow; and he that regardeth the clouds shall not reap" (Eccl. 11:4).*

Jesus felt the contrary wind when He wanted to give His life but resisted by power.

> *"Lord if it is possible let this cup be taken from me, nevertheless not my will but yours be done" (Luke 22:42).*

In other words, "I am feeling the contrary wind not to give my life, there are reasons not to, but God since it is your will I will do just that." Or don't you think He had reasons not to? I can tell you countless reasons; His mum, family, disciples, the pain, anxiety, etc. But thank God for the power to give that saw Him through.

Have you ever felt opposition or reasons not to give when you want to; these are winds you must overcome with power. Power is needed to withstand the wind and not deter from your good intention. Why is it that as soon as you begin to give, you falter and stop? Because of the opposing forces that are at work. You need the power to continue and move against the contrary wind; giving despite your prevailing needs.

Jesus said He has that power; you too can develop that power and give like He did. When you possess such power, you will be able to say yes and give whatever God lays in your heart despite challenges. Until you have that power, you will not go far in your financial destiny. Giving are the stairs to your financial destiny.

You need power not only to give, but also to give the way He wants you to give; power to pay 10% of your gross income, and even on time. Until you have the power to drop your Isaac, it abides alone. No doubt you need that power for your benefit.

Jesus Also Taught

"Give, and it shall be given unto you good measure, pressed down, shaken together and running over, shall men give unto your bosom" (Luke 6:33).

He also instructed us to lay up our treasures in heaven.

"Do not lay up for yourselves treasures on earth, where moth and rust destroy and where thieves break in and steal; 20 but lay up for yourselves treasures in heaven, where neither moth nor rust destroys and where thieves do not break in and steal. 21 For where your treasure is, there your heart will be also"(Mt. 6:19-21).

What Did Jesus Give?

Jesus was not only a teacher, but He also did what He taught. The gospel is not only an account of what of Jesus taught but also what He did.

"That which he taught, He did" (Act 1:1).

Jesus did not only teach giving, but He also gave. He gave His life and everything about Him; His glory, honour, position, riches, right, and privileges.

"who, being in the form of God, did not consider it [a]robbery to be equal with God, but [b]made Himself of no reputation, taking the form of a bondservant, and coming in the likeness of men. And being found in appearance as a man, He humbled Himself and became obedient to the point of death, even the death of the cross"(Phil 2: 6 – 8).

He gave everything about Him. He planted his life as a seed. I mean everything he did not keep anything back. He demonstrated the greatest love by giving all.

> *"Greater love hath no man than this, that a man lay down his life for his friends"(Jn. 15:13).*

What made Him give? He gave for kingdom fulfilment; to redeem and reconcile man back to God like God intends.

> *"The thief cometh not, but for to steal, and to kill, and to destroy: I am come that they might have life and that they might have it more abundantly" (Jn. 10:10).*

Jesus gave up all. What are you willing to give up to fulfil your ministry? God's call on your life is at stake. What are you willing to give up to make a people for God by your assignment?

His Reward For Giving Up This Much

He became Lord of all, King of kings. He got the final authority. Jn. 12:32

> *"Wherefore God also hath highly exalted him, and given him a name which is above every name: That at the name of Jesus every knee should bow, of things in heaven, and things in earth, and things under the earth: And that every tongue should confess that Jesus Christ is Lord, to the glory of God the Father" (Phil. 2:9-11).*

"And I, if I be lifted up from the earth, will draw all men unto me" (John 12:32).

He would have been Lord of Himself if He did not give His life. Many by their refusal to give have remained lord by themselves. Honour awaits you when you give in response to kingdom needs, and assignment. Give to move the kingdom forward for your honour.

Jesus, by His giving now has brothers, members of His body and family, even bride.

"Who is the image of the invisible God, the firstborn of every creature: For by him were all things created, that are in heaven, and that are in earth, visible and invisible, whether they be thrones, or dominions, or principalities, or powers: all things were created by him, and for him: And he is before all things, and by him all things consist. And he is the head of the body, the church: who is the beginning, the firstborn from the dead; that in all things he might have the preeminence" (Col. 1:15–18).

Could it be that the reason you are lonely is that you do not give? A giver has many friends says Solomon. Reach out to people and they will come to you, and you will have friends.

Abraham

Abraham is called the father of faith, and sure he has something to teach us his Children about giving; so we might be like him and have all his blessing. Like father, like son, they say. You cannot be proclaiming the blessing of Abraham and not care to learn from him. What made Abraham this blessed is because he was an ardent giver; to the extent of giving his only son in obedience to God. If you cannot give that your "one thing" Isaac when God demands, then you are not truly Abraham's nor entitled to all his blessing. Until you are willing to give all you have even to your "one thing," then you are not set to take all God has for you; Abraham's blessings. Abraham's blessing is not only in singing but in your willingness to give just like him.

What Did He Give?

He gave Isaac; his only hope, his long-awaited fulfilled promise. He gave precisely what God had requested. He gave in absolute obedience without compromise.

What Made Him Give?

He gave to obey God out of his love for Him. How many times have you turned back from giving what God placed in your heart to the Kingdom or to a person? That's not like your father, Abraham. Your refusal denies you of Abraham blessing. Can you give that your "one thing" to prove your love for God if he demands it? If you genuinely love him, you will obey. Giving that "one thing" is a demonstration of faith for an increase. A wise man said, when what you have is not enough, sow it as seed.

His Reward

God Provided For Him At The Same Spot

Giving that "one thing" causes the immediate release from God; His intervention. It provokes God's release. When last did you provoke God to release blessings on you? God's storehouse is full, cause a downpour by your giving.

ii). He became the father of many sons. He got his seed multiplied; gave one son and got many countless sons in fulfilment of God's promise to him. That promise of yours may be waiting to manifest by your giving.

iii). He was blessed "In blessing, I will bless you." He was eternally empowered to be blessed; endless blessing.

Solomon

Solomon built God a temple and afterwards gave an unforgettable offering.

> *"And Solomon loved the LORD, walking in the statutes of David, his father: only he sacrificed and burnt incense in high places. And the king went to Gibeon to sacrifice there;*

> *for that was the great high place: a thousand burnt offerings did Solomon offer upon that altar. In Gibeon, the LORD appeared to Solomon in a dream by night: and God said, Ask what I shall give thee" (1 Kings 3:3-5).*

Solomon did this as an expression of his love for God. God rewarded him with an open cheque and wisdom. God asked Solomon what he wanted – what a reward.

When last did you show God you love him? Sacrifice something and let God know you love him. Until you show your love sacrificially, you are not entitled to all that God has for you (an open cheque).

5. The Israelites In The Wilderness

The Israelites in the wilderness gave gold and silver even the ones on the ears of their sons and daughters. They gave these to build an ark as God commanded.

For their reward, the ark established God's presence with them for protection and preservation, which got them safely to the land of their promise; a land flowing with milk and honey. They sacrificed and got into the promised land of abundance. Without the ark, they would have been destroyed in the wilderness.

You are on a journey to your grand destiny; how much of your needs and children's are you willing to sacrifice to obey God and get to your abundance. Anything you are unwilling to sacrifice denies your abundance. How much of your needs and those of your children are you willing to trade for kingdom projects?

Your children may lack today because of your choice to meet a need in the kingdom, but I tell you their destinies are preserved. There is a promised land for your family, are you willing to sacrifice and be preserved to get there? Countless times, my children and I have denied our needs to meet Kingdom needs because we see our glorious destiny, and we have agreed not to miss it for anything.

David

> *"Now it came to pass, as David sat in his house, that David said to Nathan the prophet, Lo, I dwell in a house of cedars, but the ark of the covenant of the LORD remaineth under curtains" (1 Chronicles 17:1).*

> *"And king David said to Ornan, Nay; but I will verily buy it for the full price: for I will not take that which is thine for the LORD, nor offer burnt offerings without cost" (1 Chronicles 21:24).*

David was so much in love with God that he offered to build God a house, but God prevented him. However, he provided all that was needed for the building (1 Chron. 22:1-5, 14). You may not be a preacher, but you are willing to provide for the gospel to be preached through the appropriate media.

You may not be a writer, but you can provide for the word to be published. David was so blessed and earned the title *"Man after God's heart"* (Acts 13:32). He was committed to the fulfilment of every of God's dream. He was always seeking ways to please Him. Are you after God's heart and project? You can be sure your dream will come to pass because God will be committed to its fulfilment. God established David's throne and never abandoned him.

The Early Disciples

The early disciples gave their lives and substance; they left all to follow Jesus (Acts 2:44-47). They did this to enable the gospel to be preached everywhere (Luke 8:1-3). Without their sacrifice, the work of Jesus (Gospel) would have been stranded. You are privileged to contribute to take the gospel to the next phase and dispensation. This way, you are laying treasures in heaven where moth and rust do not destroy or thieves break in (Matt 6:19). The early disciples in reward got hundredfold of what they gave. (Mark 10:28-30).

What substance or money are you willing to part with so that God's kingdom does not suffer?

Zarephath Widow

She gave her last meal risking her life, and her son's in obedience to God's commandment (1Kings 17:8-15). She understood that when it is commanded by God, her choice was no option. Do you refuse to pay your tithe even though it is commanded? This widow risked all to obey God's command. There are instances where giving is a suggestion, and other instances, it is a commandment. Tithe and offering are commandments, they are not negotiable. It means you must give, even if it means forgoing some of your needs.

I have good news for you, God's commandments are not burdensome. When God commands you to give, it is not to punish you or deprive you but to ensure and enforce your blessing and remove devourers from you. Mark this; **any commandment to give is an enforcement to be blessed.**

"Bring ye your tithe into my storehouse...." (Mal. 3:10).

It is a command and not negotiable. Therefore align yourself with obeying it for your blessing; otherwise, you reap the consequence. God's commandment is for your benefit or curse, choose one.

The Widow's Mite

During an offering in Jesus' time, a widow gave her mite (all that she has). The Bible defines it to be all she had. Do you love God enough to give Him all that you have?

> *"And Jesus sat over against the treasury and beheld how the people cast money into the treasury: and many that were rich cast in much. And there came a certain poor widow, and she threw in two mites, which make a farthing. And he called unto him his disciples, and saith unto them, Verily I say unto you, That this poor widow hath cast more in, than all they which have cast into the treasury. For all they did cast in of their abundance; but she of her want did cast in all that she had, even all her living" (Mark 12:41-44).*

Widow's mite is the peak of giving; until you give all you have, you have not given your widow's mite. When you give your widow's mite, you receive all that God has for you. The widow gave to express appreciation to God, and she was rewarded with recognition. When last did you give that it commanded attention? When you give your widow's mite, heaven stands at attention, to deliver whatever you might need. Widow's mite is highly sacrificial.

If the above two widows gave; it simply means everyone can give when sacrifice is in place. You have not been able to give because you are unwilling to sacrifice.

Mary Magdalene

She anointed Jesus' feet with a costly fragrance to demonstrate her love, this eventually prepared Jesus for his burial. Mary Magdalene was in turn rewarded with an eternal memorial. Your gift lives you a memorial in the kingdom. There is something you have you can give for the gospel that can become a memorial for you, long after you are gone, give it now.

> *"Assuredly, I say to you, wherever this gospel is preached in the whole world, what this woman has done will also be told as a memorial to her" (Matthew 26:13).*

Time and space will fail me to continue, the list is endless. What about men and women living today, that are givers and reaping the benefits? Are you the only one left out in this list? Enlist yourself among the great by your choice to give.

Things To Note In The Above Concerning Giving:

Reward Exceeds the Gifts

So when you are asked to give, it is privileged for your increase; for turning your grain of corn into sheaves.

Note

It works regardless of age, sex, nationality, tribe, language, religion, and creed.

Sowing and harvest is spiritual law that cannot be destroyed. It stands forever. Begin to sow for the harvest of your desire.

Refusal to Give

The scripture is for your example; bad or good has something to teach. Some people refuse to give, let us examine the consequences. Good examples are the rich man in Luke 18:18-23 and the foolish man in Luke 12:16-20. (Please read those scriptures for clarity).

They paid dearly, the rich man went away sorrowful, and the foolish man paid with his life. There is no gainsaying, you cannot eat all you have, either you give to God and his kingdom for your blessing, or you give to the devil for your curse and sorrow, choose one.

I beg you, choose to give to God, meeting kingdom needs and be blessed in return. As you meet needs in the kingdom, demonstrating your love for God, you are expanding your financial destiny. Start by giving what is in your hands to move God's work in your local assembly forward. And God will definitely make all grace abound towards you (2 Cor. 9:8).

I release upon you the power to give; from today, you shall not hesitate to lay down anything God puts in your heart in Jesus' name.

My Advice

> *"Lay not up for yourselves treasures upon earth, where moth and rust doth corrupt, and where thieves break through and steal: But lay up for yourselves treasures in heaven, where neither moth nor rust doth corrupt, and where thieves do not break through nor steal: For where your treasure is, there will your heart be also" (Matthew 6:19-21).*

Lay up for yourself treasures in heaven. No doubt you have treasures here on earth, but now is the time to start laying up treasures in heaven where you will spend eternity.

What Do I Mean?

You lay up treasures in heaven by giving to kingdom work, which in turn affects souls for heaven. That soul, whose name is in the book of life is your treasure in heaven; place your priority right. God treasures the souls of men more than anything else. There is always an opportunity to save in heaven's bank for tremendous interest. Be wise and save eternally.

Resources spent on anything apart from the Kingdom such as cars, furniture, dresses, etc. are good but on themselves unwise and a great waste because it will be eaten by moths and rust. How wise are you if the bulk of your treasures are here and eventually eaten up?. Set your priorities right.

How have you supported evangelism and soul winning? Cut down on your earthly investments, consider heavenly investments. You and I are in the Kingdom today as a result of people's investments.

It is your turn to invest and move the Kingdom forward. Sacrifice and get the Kingdom going.

CHAPTER 4

Kingdom Investment

O ne significant way God brings about your desired financial destiny is by multiplying and increasing your existing resources. When the resources in your hands are multiplied and increased, you will be treading on your financial destiny.

Investment is one significant way to increase your resources. If you do not invest money, it will not grow but remains the same. But when it is invested, it yields some profit which with time abounds; establishing your financial destiny.

The same principle works in the kingdom. When you invest in the kingdom, God multiples and increases your seed. There is always return on investment in the Kingdom of God.

> *"And God is able to make all grace abound toward you; that ye, always having all sufficiency in all things, may abound to every good work: (As it is written, He hath dispersed abroad; he hath given to the poor: his righteousness remaineth for ever. Now he that ministereth seed to the sower both minister bread for your food, and multiply your seed sown, and increase the fruits of your righteousness)"*
>
> *(2 Cor. 9:8-10).*

Jesus used a grain of corn to teach His disciples this principle of multiplication in John Chapter 12.

> *"Except a grain of corn falls and dies, it abides alone" (John 12:24).*

Until you let go what is in your hands, it would not bring what you desire.

> *"Cast your bread upon the waters, for you will find it after many days" (Eccl. 11:1).*

Investment keeps your resources alive, if you do not invest and eat all you have, you will be poor. This principle is very crucial in the kingdom that Jesus likened the kingdom of God to it. He illustrated this principle in so many ways to drive home the importance of investing. Investing is like sowing and reaping.

> *"Another parable spake he unto them; The kingdom of heaven is like unto leaven, which a woman took, and hid in three measures of meal, till the whole was leavened" (Matthew 13:33).*

There is something about the kingdom that has the ability to increase your resources. In other words, the kingdom has investment capability. If this is true, then you must approach God's Kingdom with the expectation of increase.

> *"Again, the kingdom of heaven is like unto treasure hid in a field; the which when a man hath found, he hideth, and for joy thereof goeth and selleth all that he hath, and buyeth that field" (Matthew 13:44).*

This man sold all he had and bought the Kingdom; that means you must be willing to sell all you have and invest for the Kingdom to work for you. Before he sold all he had, he hid the kingdom. That means to conceal this principle in your heart, let nobody talk you out of obeying it and discourage you from investing in the Kingdom. Make up your mind, go for it, and do not entertain any doubts.

Until you hide his word and are ready to go any extent, you will not take delivery of the fullness of the Kingdom. Who says the kingdom is not costly? Get set to invest and take delivery of the richness of God's Kingdom, even your financial destiny.

"Again, the kingdom of heaven is like unto a merchant man, seeking goodly pearls" (Matthew 13:45).

I do not know what you are seeking or what might have brought you to the Kingdom, but I have good news for you, it is available only be ready to pay the price. If you really need it, then you should be prepared and willing to pay for it. Sure, this sounds like investing; which is sacrificing something you have for something (more precious) that you need.

Anyone who is not willing to invest money is not serious about his financial destiny. The true test of desire is what you are willing to pay for it. If God's kingdom is illustrated thus; that means the investment is cardinal in the kingdom. It is an essential kingdom principle. Reconsider your choice of Christianity if you are unwilling to invest your money in it.

There is no alternative; investing is the fundamental door you must walk through into God's green pasture. All you need is in the Kingdom, but you must pass through the door to obtain. This is why it is easier for the Carmel to pass through the eye of the needle than the rich to enter into the Kingdom (Matt 19:24). The Rich are people who cannot let go of what they have.

Why does the Kingdom work this way? Why must I invest to be blessed?

Investment registers your heart in the kingdom. Until your heart and life are registered in the Kingdom, you are not there and cannot access what is available. Your body may be there, but if your heart is not there, it will not work for you. Many go to church and are not blessed because their hearts are not there. They have no financial commitment to the church.

> *"For where your treasure is, there will your heart be also"* *(Mat. 6:21).*

> *"For where your treasure is, there will your heart be also"* *(Luke 12:34).*

No wonder Jesus told the rich man to sell all that he had and feed the poor (invest in the Kingdom) (Mark 10: 18 -21). Jesus simply was asking him to invest and register his heart. The kingdom is like an investment company; only the investors share the dividends.

Jesus teaches that whosoever finds the Kingdom should be willing to sell and invest in it. Be ready to part with something (and invest). Invest in soul-winning business. God depends on the funders of the kingdom to invest and move it forward. (Zechariah 1:17). God is not depending on Angels to invest in the ministry and win souls but depending on you and me.

To be a bonafide member of the kingdom, you must sell all you have to buy it; giving sacrificially. It is not a convenient kind of giving. It is the kind that is likened to investment. A farmer sows the most precious seeds and does it generously.

As you read this book, register your heart through your sacrificial giving even if you have to sell something, do it with a harvest in view. This kingdom principle is no respecter of persons; old or young, poor or rich, boy or girl, married or single. Everyone is expected to invest.

Let Us Consider Some Examples And Their Benefits:

- God invested His only Son and now has many sons and has redeemed back the earth; the silver and gold and everything else on the earth.

- Jesus invested his life, his glory, riches, wealth, and now He is Lord of Lords, and everything belongs to Him.

- The early disciples invested all they had and got hundredfold in return plus eternal life -Matthew 10:28-30, Acts 2:44-47

- Zacchaeus - Luke 19:6-9

- Lydia - Acts 16:14-15

- David

- Mary Magdalene - Mark 14:3-9

- The lad invested his five loaves of bread and two fishes - John 6:9-11

- The widow of Zarephath invested her last meal - 1Kings 17:8-16

The list is endless. Even today, many are investing and abounding in Kingdom blessing. Anything you invest in the Kingdom is blessed, multiplied, and returned to you. It may leave your hand but definitely not your life. It will surely come back to you.

You need to invest so that the Kingdom will advance and the Gospel does not die in your hands. Pass the gospel on to the next generation by your investment. Until you get involved in the gospel with your resources, you are a mere observer.

Salvation is free, but the means to spread the gospel is not free, it is costly. It cost others so much for the gospel to get to you. So be ready to pay your due to pass it on to the next person. It is a game of passing on the gospel ball by your continual investment.

2. **Why Must I Invest?**

When you invest, and souls are won, you are transferring your treasures to heaven. The souls that are won represent your resources in heaven for a heavenly blessing. When you have the blessings of heavens on your resources, they are immune to earthly hardships. When your country's economy is going down, your resources are blossoming, and you can make withdrawals.

Investing in the Kingdom expresses your love for God and His Kingdom. Until you love something, you cannot get the best out of it. Some people are merely using the Kingdom, and that is why it does not work for them. Jesus says, ***"he that does not enter through the door is a thief."*** (John 10:1). And it is impossible to steal from the kingdom; God's eye is everywhere (runs to and fro).

Love is demonstrated in giving. Love the Kingdom like David; set your affection on it, and it will work for you. You sacrifice for the one you love; sacrifice for the Kingdom and invest in it.

Like I said earlier, the principle of investment also works in the secular world. Only that investing in the Kingdom is for more exceedingly rewarding. It outweighs every other investment.

Investing In The Kingdom Has A Lot Of Advantages

- It is guaranteed. (**Matthew 6:21, Luke 12:34**). There is no uncertainty or fraud.

- God, the Chief Executive Officer of kingdom business, is able and omnipotent. He is all powerful and can do anything, and He can multiply every seed sown (2 Corinthians. 9:6-12).

- The profit rate is overwhelming. It is a hundred-fold increase. It is like investing a grain of corn and getting sheaves of corn (**Mark10:30, Luke 6:38, Psalms 126:5-6**).

- There are also fringe benefits that come with the return. Examples are Joy, Righteousness, Grace, Breakthrough, etc.

- What you invest in the kingdom never dies because the kingdom is eternal. It abides even to your fourth generation.

Maximizing Your Investment

If you want to get the best out of your investment, there are things you must know and do. Attitude is everything; it matters in all we do. If you need to maximize your investment, you must have the right attitude. Attitude provides the proper condition for your seed to yield tremendously.

The basis of every giving in the Kingdom should be love. Love should be what is motivating you to give.

> *"For God so loved the world, that he gave his only begotten Son, that whosoever believeth in him should not perish, but have everlasting life." (John 3:16).*

Let love for God and the kingdom be the only motivating factor for your giving. God is not your heavenly banker but your heavenly father. He is not a money doubler but a father who blesses. God only responds to giving when He sees love.

> *"Because he hath set his love upon me, therefore will I deliver him: I will set him on high because he hath known my name. He shall call upon me, and I will answer him: I will be with him in trouble; I will deliver him, and honour him. With long life will I satisfy him, and shew him my salvation" (Psalms 91:14-16).*

God desires a loving relationship with you than your resources. No wonder, He says, *"My son give me your heart."* (Prov. 23:26a). You must first give God your heart before your money. For every giving to yield profit, first of all, give your heart. Be passionate about Him; loving Him with all your heart, strength, and soul. When you do; you will give excitedly. When you grumble or murmur at the announcement to give; the love is not in your heart, and I advise you to have a change of attitude before giving.

"God loves and reward cheerful giver" (2 Cor. 9:7b).

When you are in love, you are excited to give and even look for more reasons to give. I know how it feels to be in love, every occasion or event is enough reason to give that you forget your needs. Until you get to this point with God; looking out for opportunities to give, your investment will not yield fully. God detests when you give grudgingly or out of necessity; as though you are being forced to give.

Lack of love for God hinders you from giving your best, and this is unacceptable to God. Malachi 1 describes it as polluted offerings. Abel offered to God out of love. Love motivated him to give his best, which God accepted. Cain's giving was rejected and did not yield any benefits.

If you love God, you will not continue in the sin the Lord convicts you of because you want to please Him and not hurt Him. (John 14:15). Obeying God keeps us away from sin makes our giving effective. If you are unwilling to put off the old man (nature), please reconsider your investing in the kingdom because God cannot be mocked. You can mock (deceive) men but not God. Lying, cheating, anger, malice, bitterness, pride, envy, fornication, adultery, and such likes are the little foxes that eat up what you invest. Get rid of them before investing if you desire a great harvest. This is also breaking up the fallow ground, not sowing among thorns. Thorns are sins in your lives that choke your seed from being fruitful; preventing a bumper harvest.

Jesus taught to keep your offering and reconcile with your brother and afterwards bring it to guarantee a harvest.

> *"Therefore if thou bring thy gift to the altar, and there rememberest that thy brother hath ought against thee; Leave there thy gift before the altar, and go thy way; first be reconciled to thy brother, and then come and offer thy gift"* *(Matt. 5:23-24).*

Check your obedience to the word. If you have been investing and not harvest much, examine your ways. If you are not ready to change your ways and begin to obey God; do not bother wasting your resources by investing it into the kingdom.

Sins in people's lives make it seem that the Kingdom is not working. You must break your fallow ground and get rid of sins. Allow the word to change you.

> *"They do not say in their heart, "Let us now fear the Lord our God, Who gives rain, both the former and the latter, in its*

season. He reserves for us the appointed weeks of the harvest."
Your iniquities have turned these things away, and your sins
have withheld good from you" (Jeremiah 5:24-25 NKJV).

No matter the weight of your investment, you should
fear God and be subject to His Lordship.

He must be the shepherd and you the sheep to access
the pasture for your harvest. You must be His child in
character, behaviour, and word to be entitled to His
pasture. **(Jer. 8:20).** Until I decided to change, the
kingdom did not profit me.

> *"Nevertheless the foundation of God standeth sure, having*
> *this seal, The Lord knoweth them that are his. And, Let every*
> *one that nameth the name of Christ depart from iniquity" (2*
> *Tim. 2:19).*

> *"My son give me your heart and lay my commandment in*
> *your heart" (Prov. 7:1).*

Only love connects your heart to God for your harvest.
Any giving outside love does not profit you because there
is no heart connection. Your offering and investment is
detestable and wearies God without demonstrating love
and demonstrated obedience to His word.

> *"And ye shall seek me, and find me when ye shall search for me*
> *with all your heart" (Jeremiah 29:13).*

Love makes you find God and connect to Him for your reward. Investing stolen money into the kingdom is an abomination to God or money from adultery or fornication, ill-gotten wealth is detestable, and you cannot be blessed by such.

I know that this chapter has opened your eyes to the investment capability of God's kingdom and how you can maximize it.

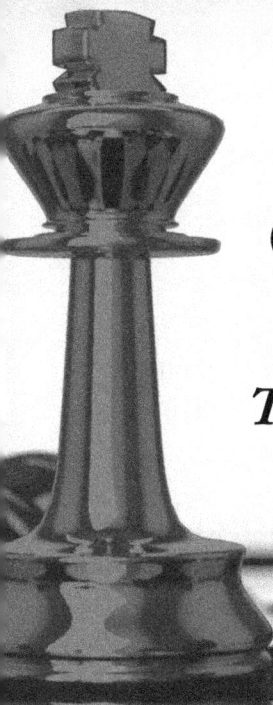

CHAPTER 5

Tithe and Offering

Kingdom investment is one major way to multiply your resources for financial destiny. The kingdom has investment capability, able to multiply the resources you saved. There are different ways to invest in the kingdom; tithe and offering, giving to the servants of God, kingdom project, etc.

Tithe and Offering

We shall be looking at tithe and offering:

- What is Tithe?

- Where do you pay Tithe To?

- What Tithe is not?

- Benefits of Tithing.

Tithe

A tithe is 10% of your income. For every pay cheque, God expects you to invest back 10% of it into His kingdom so that there will be meat (provision, resources) to meet the needs in the kingdom.

> *"Bring the whole tithe into the storehouse, that there may be food in my house. Test me in this," says the Lord Almighty, "and see if I will not throw open the floodgates of heaven and pour out so much blessing that there will not be room enough to store it" Malachi 3:10" (NIV).*

Although the tithe belongs to God, when you pay it; He blesses and multiples your resources. Through your tithe, overhead costs of the church; rent and other bills are paid, including administrative bills. Your tithe not only meets the needs of the church, but it is also an expression of your appreciation to God, for His partnership with you at work to make wealth.

> *"But remember the Lord your God, for it is he who gives you the ability to produce wealth, and so confirms his covenant, which he swore to your ancestors, as it is today" (Deuteronomy 8:18).*

By tithing, you appreciate God for strength, wisdom, and grace He has given you for your work.

The reason you got that money is that God gave you the power to make it; otherwise, it would not have been possible. Your tithe is God's portion of your pay cheque, that is why it is a commandment and not negotiable. It is God's share for been involved in your work. You must bring your tithe, or you are a thief; robbing God.

If God demanded 10% from the Old Testament believers, I am sure He demands even more from us whom He has redeemed through his son. For whom much is given, much is expected. My understanding of this made me decide long ago not to only pay tithe but even more. If you are struggling with paying your tithe, re-examine your Salvation and Christianity. If the kingdom must profit you, you must be a bonafide member by your tithing.

Tithe is God's portion and is to be brought into His house. It is not yours to dispense as you wish, it should not be used by you or outside the church. Tithe is not to be used as philanthropy. (Deuteronomy 14:24-25). Tithe is to be brought to the house of God for kingdom work. Your tithe is for the expansion of the kingdom so that the earth may be filled with the glory of God as waters cover the sea.

When you pay your tithe, the kingdom moves on, and it blesses people. Without your tithe, the work of the kingdom is stagnated.

Some Scriptural References To Validate Tithing

- Abraham paid tithe: Genesis 14:20, Genesis 28:22.

- Tithe is due to God: Leviticus 27:30, Proverbs 3:9, Malachi 3:8.

- Tithe was granted to the Levites: Numbers 18:21, 2 Chronicles 31:5, Nehemiah 10:37, Hebrew 7:4-8, Deuteronomy 14:22-25.

Who Pays Tithe?

Everyone is expected to tithe because the earth is the Lord, and we all dwell in it. Individuals, communities, nations, churches, businesses, and every income generating venture should pay tithe. God expects every dweller of the earth to pay tithe to Him.

Benefits of Tithing

Your tithing makes you enjoy the blessings of God

> *"Prove me in this, if I will not open the windows of Heaven and pour out such blessing......" (Malachi 3:10-12).*

Tithing keeps the windows of heaven open above you; makes you operate under an open heaven.

"The Lord will open to you His good [a]treasure, the heavens, to give the rain to your land in its season, and to bless all the work of your hand. You shall lend to many nations, but you shall not borrow" (Deuteronomy 28:12 NKJV).

When the window of heaven is opened, it rains. Rain signifies the presence of the Holy Spirit that brings blessings, inspirations, ideas, insights, etc. When you pay your tithe; God gives you insights to excel in your job and stand out.

He gives you inspiration and ideas to increase you. This might be an idea to do something new. When God's idea is implemented, it yields so much. An idea from God is enough to turn your life around.

Tithing Empowers You To Succeed

Blessing means empowerment to succeed. God will not only give you ideas, But He also ensures you succeed. God's blessing ensures that your business plans and vision succeed and not get aborted or die. It is not enough to have a plan; you need the power to bring it to pass for profit.

Could it be that the reason you are not making a way in that business is because of your refusal to pay tithe? You should not wait until everything is ok to tithe, if you begin to pay your tithe now, power will be released to make it alright.

Tithe puts a blessing on you so that whatever you lay your hands to do prospers so much "…..that there will not be room enough to receive it"(Mal. 3:10).

Tithing Rebukes Devourers For Your Sake

Not only does tithing increase you, but it also ensures your protection. God, through your tithe, ensures that you and your blessing are safe and secured, and there is no breaking-in.

Tithe Makes All Nations To Call You Blessed

That means you are blessed wherever you go, in any nation you find yourself, even in a strange land. When you tithe, your desire in every nation will be granted to you. The land shall yield her increase for you.

Tithe makes God's blessing upon you not to be limited geographically. Do you want to possess any land you tread upon and take delivery of what is yours? Pay your tithe. If you do not tithe, things become tight. God is the God of all the earth when you connect to Him by your tithe; you enjoy the fruit of all the earth.

Tithe Establishes The Fear Of God In You

> *"And thou shalt eat before the LORD thy God, in the place which he shall choose to place his name there, the tithe of thy corn, of thy wine, and of thine oil, and the firstlings of thy herds*

and of thy flocks; that thou mayest learn to fear the LORD thy God always" (Deuteronomy 14:23).

When you tithe, it establishes the fear of God in you; which is your security.

What Happens If I Do Not Tithe?

"Will a man rob God? Yet ye have robbed me. But ye say Wherein have we robbed thee? In tithes and offerings. Ye are cursed with a curse: for ye have robbed me, even this whole nation" (Malachi 3:8-9).

If you refuse to tithe, you are cursed; empowered to fail. You make yourself out to be a thief and curses abide in the house of a thief. If you do not pay your tithe, you are robbing God of His share and frustrating His grace in your life. When God's grace is frustrated, you are defeated.

Curses prevail in the absence of grace. Devourers come in to eat your blessing; putting holes in your pockets, your money goes without reasonable accounting. Note this: if you do not pay tithe to God, you are unconsciously paying it to the devil, and I assure you it will be far more than 10%.

How You May Ask?

Through medical bills, car repairs, accidents, lawyer fees, and other unbudgeted expenses. No man can eat all he earns, either you pay tithe to God or to the devil. Choose who you pay to.

I advise you; pay to God because He rewards with so many benefits. Moreover, the devil will demand way more than 10%. If you are in a financial crisis, you might be paying so much to the devil. Repent now.

Tithe paying is so essential that in the Old Testament when a man pays it late, he had to add a 5% interest. Tithing should be consistent not on and off or whenever it is convenient. It should be paid on time, not late. You should not use your tithe for something else to pay later. As soon as your pay cheque arrives, pay your tithe.

Tithe is a spiritual law for your blessing as it ensures open heavens over you. Do not close the heaven over you by your refusal to tithe. You cannot bear the gravity of operating under closed heavens.

If you own a business, pay the tithe, and you will be amazed at the blessings God will bring to you.

I believe after this chapter, tithing will never be a struggle to you; that you will excitedly pay your tithe. The blessing of tithing will abound in your life because the heaven above you is open.

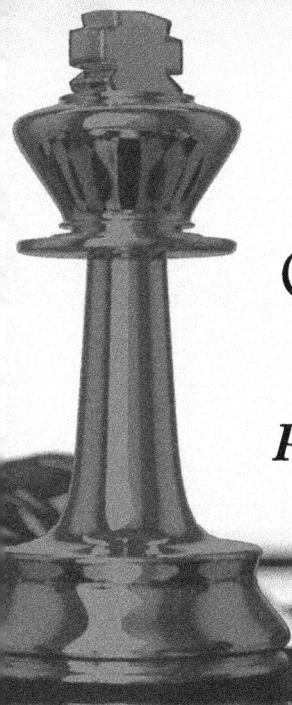

CHAPTER 6

Prophets Offering

I f you desire financial increase, you must be an investor
in the kingdom of God. It is by investing your present
resources that God multiplies it and makes it abound
for your financial destiny.

> *"And God is able to make all grace abound toward you; that*
> *ye, always having all sufficiency in all things, may abound*
> *to every good work: (As it is written, He hath dispersed*
> *abroad; he hath given to the poor: his righteousness*
> *remaineth for ever. Now he that ministereth seed*
> *to the sower both minister bread for your food, and*

multiply your seed sown, and increase the fruits of your righteousness" (2 Cor. 9: 8-10).

One way to invest in the kingdom is by giving to the man or woman of God; who preaches the word to you. Today, this is the most neglected aspect of giving in the kingdom. Believers do not see the need to invest in their pastors, forgetting that it is their responsibilities to give to their pastors.

When you give to the man or woman of God, you are investing because God will multiply it and give it back to you. In as much as you pay your tithe, are involved in kingdom projects, let something leave you and go to the servant of God as an investment.

> *"But I rejoiced in the Lord greatly that now, at last, you care for me has flourished again; though you surely did care, but you lacked opportunity. ...Not that I seek the gift, but I seek the fruit that abounds to your account. Indeed I [e]have all and abound. I am full, having received from Epaphroditus the things sent from you, a sweet-smelling aroma, an acceptable sacrifice, well pleasing to God. And my God shall supply all your need according to His riches in glory by Christ Jesus"* Phil. 4: 10-19 (NKJV).

> *"Blessed are you who sow beside all waters, Who send out freely the feet of the ox and the donkey"Isaiah 32:20 (NKJV).*

These scriptures refer to the reward of investing in the lives of God's servants. The Philippians ministered to Paul's need, and they reaped this prayer as their reward.

"My Lord shall supply all your needs according to His riches by Christ Jesus." (Phil. 4:19).

When you invest in the servant of the Lord, the Lord multiplies and supplies your needs. The widow invested her last meal in the servant of God, God multiplied her resources, and she entered her financial destiny. She and her son would have died of famine if she did not invest.

God's servants are special to God. They are God's servant and messengers. They are God's representatives, therefore, when you give (invest) to them, you are provoking God to cause a release on you. Also by your giving, you appreciate God for His gift of them.

"He that receiveth a prophet in the name of a prophet shall receive a prophet's reward; and he that receiveth a righteous man in the name of a righteous man shall receive a righteous man's reward. And whosoever shall give to drink unto one of these little ones a cup of cold water only in the name of a disciple, verily I say unto you, he shall in no wise lose his reward" (Matt. 10:41-42).

Who is a Prophet?

A prophet is God's mouthpiece that God uses to speak to you and bless your life. He is a channel of spiritual blessing and impartation. Every promise of God is voice activated, especially by His Prophet. God powers and informs the words and counsel of His messenger, the Prophet.

How To Receive A Prophet

By giving him a cup of cold water. What does cold water signify? Water comes to meet a particular need; thirst. Therefore giving a cup of water to a Prophet signifies meeting a specific need in his life.

Note: Cold water, not warm or hot water. That talks about the wholesome, fresh, and worthwhile gift that meets his need. In order words, to receive a prophet means relating to a prophet to meet a particular need in his or her life; you are connecting to him by your giving.

Why Give To A Prophet?

- **He Is A Gift To You From God**

    "He that descended is the same also that ascended up far above all heavens, that he might fill all things.) And he gave some, apostles; and some, prophets; and some, evangelists; and some, pastors and teachers" (Eph. 4: 10-11).

You cannot buy him, but you can appreciate him with your gifts.

"Verily, verily, I say unto you, He that receiveth whomsoever I send receiveth me; and he that receiveth me receiveth him that sent me" (John 13:20).

- ### *You Give To A Prophet Because It Is His Right And Reward*

"Whoever goes to war at his own expense? Who plants a vineyard and does not eat of its fruit? Or who tends a flock and does not drink of the milk of the flock?·· Even so, the Lord has commanded that those who preach the gospel should live from the gospel" 1Cor. 9: 7-14 (NKJV).

He ministers spiritual things to you. He that preaches the word should live by the word. He threshes the corn of God's word for your blessing so, he should not be muzzled. It is wickedness not to bless the servant of God. God is the witness if he does his part; preaching the word, he should not be denied of his reward. If he ministers spiritual things to you, in response, you should share your material blessings with him.

It is not enough for you to be blessed by him, you should respond to him by your giving. God expects something to leave you to His servant on a regular basis as long as he ministers to you, or you will be muzzling the ox that treads the corn and that is wickedness and a show of ingratitude.

Have you been a blessing to your pastor lately? Repent and start reaching out to him on a regular basis. You may say; but I pay my tithe and offering, but those are not for him. He pays tithe too. The tithe and offering is for the ministry and run by church personnel other than the servant of God; it is not his money.

If God is using your pastor to bless you, let him use you to bless him in return. Only then will the circuit be complete. This is the reason why blessings are lacking in many churches because the circle is broken.

When You Give To The Servant Of God, It Shows Your Acceptance And Belief In Him

Your gift simply says "I believe you and your message and I plant my heart and life to receive it". Where your treasure is there your heart is also. Only then can you receive the true blessing he carries or brings to you. The reason why the word works for some and do not for others could be their inability to relate to the vessel that preaches the word, planting their hearts to receive it.

When your heart is connected by your gift, every word the Prophet or Pastor speaks will find expression in your life. Nothing connects hearts than gifts. Your heart is not connected to your pastor because you are a worker or leader in your church but by your gift to him.

Amongst all the churches Paul started, the only church that was connected to him to receive his reward was the Philippians church.

"Now you Philippians know also that in the beginning of the gospel, when I departed from Macedonia, no church shared with me concerning giving and receiving but you only. For even in Thessalonica you sent aid once and again for my necessities. Not that I seek the gift, but I seek the fruit that abounds to your account. Indeed I [a]have all and abound. I am full, having received from Epaphroditus the things sent from you, a sweet-smelling aroma, an acceptable sacrifice, well pleasing to God. And my God shall supply all your need according to His riches in glory by Christ Jesus" (Philippians 4:15-19 NKJV).

When you connect to the heart of God's servant, prayers naturally flows from him to God on your behalf ceaselessly and God in turn blesses you. This is a spiritual principle as well as natural principle. Though you may even be related to him as a wife or child; you must employ this principle to be blessed.

Isaac loved Esau but demanded venison so that his heart could bless him.

"Isaac said, "I am old. Maybe I will die soon. So take your bow and arrows and go hunting. Kill an animal for me to eat. Prepare the food that I love. Bring it to me, and I will eat it. Then I will bless you before I die" (Genesis 27:2-4 ERV).

For an effectual blessing; the heart must be provoked and one major way is through giving. When the pastor's heart is not provoked or stirred, there is no effectual blessing. This is one of the reasons many church folks are not financially blessed.

Are you presently going through challenges? Explore this principle. I tell you, only one genuine prayer from your pastor is all you need for a turn around. All the prayers you have been receiving from your pastors have not been working because you did not provoke an effectual one by your giving nor connected with your heart.

No wonder in the Old Testament people do not go to a prophet without a gift. This is not bribery but a spiritual and natural law to stir up his heart for effectual blessing.

> *"But the servant answered, "A man of God is in this town. People respect him. Everything he says comes true, so let's go into town. Maybe the man of God will tell us where we should go next." Saul said to his servant, "Sure, we can go into town, but what can we give to him? We have no gift to give the man of God. Even the food in our bags is gone. What can we give him?" Again the servant answered Saul. "Look, I have a little bit of money.[a] Let's give it to the man of God. Then he will tell us where we should go" (1 Samuel 9:6-8 ERV).*

Your pastor may be genuine in his prayer for you, but if your heart is not there by your gift, you will not obtain the blessing. More so as you plant yourself in his life by your gift, you become valuable to kingdom vision and he will give everything to see you fulfilled and satisfied. He gives his life as a good shepherd to keep you safe.

Paul was asking the people to give so that it may abound in their accounts. When you give to the servant of God, it abounds to your account for you to withdraw when you need it.

You Are Giving To Your Pastor Because It Is A Commandment?

In the Old Testament, the Levites had no field and their fellow brothers were commanded by God to give to them from their harvest. Priesthood unto God was their portion. **(Josh.18:7, Josh.13:14, Josh.21:3)**. By God's design, His servants were not to do other work but be fully dedicated to Him. He was their portion.

Today, people's reluctance to give to servants of God has sent God's servants into the streets fending for themselves. As a result, they do not find the time to thresh the corn in prayer and the word to feed the sheep and the sheep suffers, there is no appreciable growth in their ministries. What a viscous circle; God forbid. When you give to God's servant, it is for your good. Begin to give to your pastors so that ministry will be done according to God's design for your own profit.

When things are done as God commands, the profit will be enjoyed by all. Know this; if you refuse to give to the man of God, you will lose your blessing, but God will raise someone to bless His servant. He is God's servant and he is God's responsibility. God is not limited on who to use to bless his servant but if you allow Him use you, He will bless you. He will multiply what you gave and give it back to you.

What Do I Give?

What you give to the servant of God may be as cheap as a cup of water but let it be cold; wholesome and fresh, meeting a particular need. What you give should be wholesome and acceptable, presented in a cup; in a manner to be accepted. Give in humility not in arrogance; consider it a privilege to give to the servant of God. He is God's servant not your servant, so do it with respect and honour, well packaged. Do not squeeze the dollar bills into his hands, put it in an envelope, addressed and properly delivered.

Remember it must be cold water, wholesome and fresh. If you want to give clothing, do not give old worn out clothes of many years ago, warm water is not acceptable. Give something that God would be pleased and reward you for because you are actually giving to God. Give something worthwhile because he is a prophet and not a beggar. Give him in the name of a prophet not in the name of a beggar.

Do not give her something you condemned that is worthless, you are not giving because she lacks nor begging but for your blessing. So give something you will be happy to receive when God multiplies it and returns to you. Give sacrificially. Give your pastor in the name of a prophet not in the name of a beggar or underprivileged and you will receive a good reward.

Areas To Give

Like I said earlier, you give to meet specific needs. Watch out for needs in his or her life and give appropriately.

These Could Come Through:

- *Your Desire*

What do you want the servant of God to have which you can afford or sacrifice to get; this could be an indication of what to give him or her. Even if you cannot afford it now, you can believe God to enable you to do that for His servant. If God sees it in your heart for His servant, He will put it in your hands as a seed. Until then give the little you can afford. I tell you; nothing is too big for Gods servant. Let your value be right.

- *The Area You Could Give To Your Pastor May Come As A Burden*

If you are displeased with an area in your pastor's life; it is an indication of what to give. If you do not like his dresses, God might be leading you to invest in that. Supply that cup of water to meet that particular need in his or her life. Whenever I felt burdened by any area of the servants of God I have been privileged to work with; I went out of my way to meet that need. Most times I sacrifice to do this.

How many times have you pushed away the burden you have to do one thing or the other for your pastor? I tell you, you pushed away your opportunities to be blessed. I closely observe my pastor for areas of lack or need to meet it. These needs might be in him, his wife or kids. Keep your eyes open on your pastor and his family, they are your responsibility and God will show you a need to meet in his or her life.

Purpose to be a channel to bless your pastor or any servant of God you are privileged to know and God will bless you in return. When you do this an account will abound on your behalf.

- **There Are Other Ways To Give**

Give your word to encourage him or her as she labours. Give your obedience to support him. Give your time and energy to help at home especially e.g. babysitting.

Whatever form you can reach out to your pastor is honoured by God.

What Do I Gain By Giving To My Pastor?

You gain prophet reward; apart from God multiplying the seed sown and giving it back to you, you receive the prophet's reward. Your blessing is 2 folds; God's reward and prophet's reward. God blesses as the man of God pronounces blessings on you. The blessing of the servant of God is the prophet's reward.

Every servant of God is a package of gifts and blessing to mankind. They carry different gifts and blessings. Every servant of God carries specific reward; package of gifts and blessings. I want you to see the servant of God as container of gifts and when you receive him, he in turn off loads the gifts on you.

Servant of God is a carrier of God's grace and gifts, when you are connected for the flow of God's grace and gift in his life, you will soon notice that the gifts that operates in your pastor's life is working in yours too. This is very true in my life. Every servant of God I have been privileged to give, I find out that the grace and gifts that operate in his or her life is working in my life. For me; that's one of the prophet's rewards.

If there is a gift you admire in your pastor, you can begin now to sow towards that; connecting your heart for it. There is no gift or grace you need from God that is not in a vessel especially the one He has sent to you (your pastor). Tap into it by your regular and sacrificial giving regardless of your relationship with him or her. If spiritual destiny is your goal, there is something in your pastor you need, that is why God has sent him to you. Identify it and begin to connect your heart for a flow. It is not in wishing but in giving.

I say this boldly, the gift and grace of God I operate today are products of my giving to the servants of God I have been privileged to work with. There is virtually no servant of God I meet that I did not connect with and contract grace from, and today those gifts and grace are speaking and establishing my destiny.

If you do not know; your pastor carries precious gifts and grace of God that you need to be established. Begin to connect with it and not too long it will be evident in your life. Your gifts make room for you and bring you before great men. God says *"If I am your father, where is my honour?"* (Mal. 1:6). Honour your spiritual fathers and mothers with your gifts and be impacted. I tell you this is one of the kingdom mysteries for your prosperity.

You are highly privileged to read these, it is not a prank, it works.

You Have To Watch Out For These Or Your Benefit Will Be Denied:

- Never give for a wrong motive.

You are not giving to control, dictate or boss your pastor.

- Never give and turn around and backbite him. That's hypocrisy, it does not work that way. Sincere love should be in your heart for your gift to be rewarded and be a blessing to you.

- Disobedience to the word he preaches or the assignment he commits to you nullifies your reward.

- Strive and competition. Do not give as competition with another person or to get a position, give to your pastor as a service towards God and then looking to God for reward. Do not give to win a position or opportunity. Once you are approved by God, He places you in a befitting position. For promotion does not come from man but from God.

"For exaltation comes neither from the east Nor from the west nor from the south. But God is the Judge: He puts down one, And exalts another" (Psalms 75:6-7).

Your pastor is sent for your good, receive him and you will be blessed. God has seen your affliction and has sent a deliverer and helper in the person of His servant, your pastor. RECEIVE HIM.

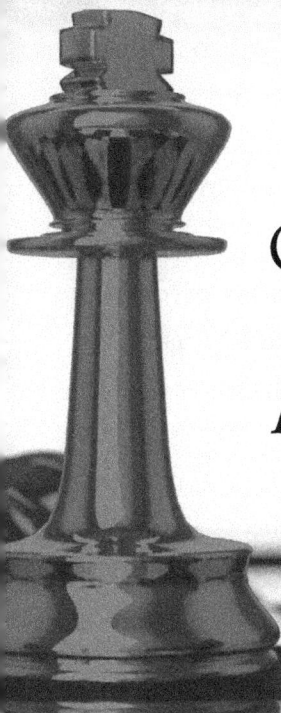

CHAPTER 7

Kingdom Project

In the previous chapters, there has been an emphasis on Kingdom investment, explaining the fact that God's Kingdom has kingdom investment capabilities that can multiply the resources you invested in it. One of the significant ways to invest in the kingdom is through financing Kingdom projects.

Note: there are many more ways to invest in the kingdom other than the ones mentioned in this book. Until you discover the purpose of finance; supply will be limited and abuse inevitable. Abuse of finance is the reason why a onetime rich fellow suddenly becomes poor and begging. They abuse finance, and it runs from them. (Read Luke 12:13-21).

The rich man in this story thought that the essence of wealth was for him to be merry and please himself, but that is wrong. Today; many still think that way, and on their list, they do not have anything else other than self. In this chapter, you will understand the essence that God wants to establish you financially, and as you begin to operate, thereby you will increase. David understood this and was established.

"And in my prosperity I said, I shall never be moved" (Psalms 30:6).

The reason God sends financial increase to you is for you to be rich towards Him.

"So is he who lays up treasure for himself, and is not rich toward God" (Luke 12:21).

The resources in your hands are seeds God has given you to sow for Him to multiply and return to you. If you give to the Kingdom, you are rich towards God and will have all your needs met. The reason God blesses you financially is to be rich towards Him; to give back to Him through building His kingdom.

God's Principles of Obtaining Financial Miracles 90

"For thus says the Lord of hosts: 'Once more (it is a little while) I will shake heaven and earth, the sea and dry land; 7 and I will shake all nations, and they shall come to the] Desire of All Nations, and I will fill this temple with glory,' says the Lord of hosts. 'The silver is Mine, and the gold is Mine,' says the Lord of hosts. 'The glory of this latter temple shall be greater than the former,' says the Lord of hosts.'And in this place, I will give peace,' says the Lord of hosts" (Haggai 2:6-9 NKJV).

"And I told them of the hand of my God which had been good upon me, and also of the king's words that he had spoken to me. So they said, "Let us rise up and build." Then they set[a] their hands to this good work. But when Sanballat the Horonite, Tobiah the Ammonite official, and Geshem the Arab heard of it, they laughed at us and despised us, and said, "What is this thing that you are doing? Will you rebel against the king?" So I answered them, and said to them, "The God of heaven Himself will prosper us; therefore we, His servants will arise and build, but you have no heritage or right or memorial in Jerusalem" (Nehemiah 2:18-20).

When your heart is genuinely set to build God's house, He sends finances to you. When it is in your heart to build His kingdom, He puts the resources you need in your hands. God has a vision for His Church, and He depends on you and me to channel the resources He has sent to achieve it.

God wants the gospel to be permeate every sphere if life. He wants His kingdom extended to every place. In any work of the Kingdom you are part of, channel your resources to advance it.

> **"Cry yet, saying, Thus saith the LORD of hosts; My cities through prosperity shall yet be spread abroad, and the LORD shall yet comfort Zion, and shall yet choose Jerusalem" (Zech. 1:17).**

God wants His church to be outstanding to gain attraction, such that people will long to be associated with it. Compare where your local assembly is now to where God wants it to be; I think there are still more to be done. Get set to build, and God will prosper you.

If you are involved in a new ministry, you are privileged – because it is an opportunity to be blessed unto your financial destiny. When your heart is set to build the kingdom, God supplies the money needed. When you partake in realising God's vision, you will be lifted.

God Is Counting On You To Build His Kingdom: (Heb. 3:4, Hag. 1:8).

He expects you to sacrifice; going the extra mile to build. When God wanted the Israelites to build an Ark in the wilderness, He commanded Moses to take an offering from anyone whose heart was willing. (**Exodus 25:1-9, Exodus 35:4-9, 20-29, Exodus 39:32-42**).

Involvement in kingdom project is not by compulsion. Look out for what is needed in your church and supply it. Nehemiah and his men realised kingdom project needs. It does not matter how feeble you might seem financially when your heart is in building, you are strengthened to build. (**Nehemiah 2:17-20**).

Blessings of Building the Kingdom

• It establishes God's presence with you.

When people complete the project God commanded, it establishes God's presence with them in a higher dimension. After the Israelites built the temple, the presence of God was manifested more. Also, when the Ark was completed, God honoured it with His presence. The presence of God is richly conveyed when a kingdom project is completed. He is glorified and honoured; and when God is honoured, blessings flow.

> *"....and in this place will I give peace, saith the LORD of hosts" (Haggai 2:9b).*

> *"So he built the house, and finished it, and covered the house with beams and boards of cedar. And then he built chambers against all the house, five cubits high: and they rested on the house with timber of cedar. And the word of the LORD came to Solomon, saying, Concerning this house which thou art in building, if thou wilt walk in my statutes, and execute my judgments, and keep all my commandments to walk in them; then will I perform my word with thee, which I spake unto David thy father: And I will dwell among the children of Israel, and will not forsake my people Israel. So Solomon built the house and finished it" (1Kings 6:9-14).*

For every kingdom project, God commands you to embark on, He has the purpose of blessing His people. And after the project is realized, He releases the blessing. You limit God's blessing in your life if you are not committed to Kingdom project. Kingdom project is from phase to phase, stage to stage, and as you get committed to realising it, you move from glory to glory in your blessing.

There was glory associated with the building of the Ark, and that was related to the building of the Temple. Do not be tired. Be involved in every project and abound in blessing. The several projects in your local assembly are packages for your blessing, so embrace each one with excitement.

> *"Give a portion to seven, and also to eight; for thou knowest not what evil shall be upon the earth." (Ecclesiastes 11:2).*

There is a blessing for you in God, but you must provoke it by your commitment to kingdom project.

> *"Now it came to pass, when Isaac was old and his eyes were so dim that he could not see, that he called Esau his older son and said to him, "My son" and he answered him, "Here I am." Then he said, "Behold now, I am old. I do not know the day of my death. Now therefore, please take your weapons, your quiver and your bow, and go out to the field and hunt game for me. And make me [a]savory food, such as I love, and bring it to me that I may eat, that my soul may bless you before I die" (Gen. 27:1-4 NKJV).*

Real blessing comes from the heart. Until the heart is stirred it cannot bless. Therefore, a wise person seeks what to do in order to stir for the release of blessings. Whenever God demands something from you, it is for His spirit to be stirred into, you. It is you that needs God, so seek to touch and stir His heart for your blessing. Whether you are involved in the project or not, God's work will still go on, so humble yourself and seek His face. This may be harsh but it is true.

I always keep in mind that God can do without me but I cannot do without Him. It is me that needs Him, so I comply with His will. God has given you open cheque; cash it by your commitment to kingdom project. You are giving to God for your blessings; you are not giving to men.

Consequences Of Not Committing To Kingdom Project

Does everyone get involved in kingdom project? No. Only the wise, whose hearts are willing to get involved. Those that refuse to be involved suffer.

- In Moses' time, the people that did not give their gold to the building of the Ark gave it for the golden calf that destroyed them.

- In Nehemiah's time, the noble (proud and arrogant) did not build; when the wall was completed they were disheartened.

"And it happened, when all our enemies heard of it, and all the nations around us saw these things, that they were very disheartened in their own eyes; for they perceived that this work was done by our God" (Nehemiah 6:16 NKJV).

With or without them, the noble, the work still went on. God said *"I will build my church, and the gates of hell shall not prevail against it"* (Matt 16:18). You cannot hold God to ransom with your money, keep your money and the project will still go on and be completed.

Are you a noble in the kingdom, who feels he can hold God's work to ransom? God shall prosper His people, and they shall build. Some are too noble that even after the teaching from God's word, they still refuse to pay tithe, filled with their own ways. Tell me what is higher than God's word?

I advise you lay aside all superfluity of naughtiness and receive with meekness the engrafted word which is able to save your soul. If you do not pay tithe nor committed to kingdom project, you are a noble and God is not counting on you to build His kingdom. Repent for your blessing. Nobles are made up on their ways, too noble to change their views. In the kingdom, it must not be your way, but the King's way. It is unrealistic to think that everyone in the kingdom is committed to the work. If you want to build, then resolve that no one corrupts you and takes you away from your destination.

There is a danger of not being involved in the work of the kingdom. (**Haggai 1:2-11, Luke 12:13-20, Matthew 10:21-22**).

Anything you cannot let go when God demands it for kingdom project becomes source of sorrow to you. Do not use that money you set aside for kingdom project, do not even use it on your children. Never use the gold God demands on your children or they will be a source of sorrow for you.

For every project you get involved as a family, God moves you on to a higher level. As a family, do not spend that which is God's and save your family from the undue curse. Eli paid dearly for this. Do not honour your children more than God. Do you have money to do everything for your children and none for God? This is honouring your children above God. Remember children are gifts and rewards from God. That means honouring the giver more than the gift.

Today this is brought to your attention so that those gifts of children will not be cursed. You cannot separate the gift from the giver. If you want the gift to be beneficial and useful, you must esteem the giver by your right attitude, through giving.

"Wherefore the LORD God of Israel saith, I said indeed that thy house, and the house of thy father, should walk before me forever: but now the LORD saith, Be it far from me; for them that honour me I will honour, and they that despise me shall be lightly esteemed" (1 Sam. 2:30).

God's promises are hanging over your family, so honour God and teach every member to, and you will realise the blessings. Do not compromise giving to God; honour God with your substance. Be involved in kingdom project even if it means forfeiting a need *"the poor you always have with you"* Jesus said.

Do not let any opportunity pass by. Cash on it. Do not be deprived of your blessing.

CHAPTER 8

Covenant By Sacrifice

"The mighty God, even the LORD, hath spoken and called the earth from the rising of the sun unto the going down thereof. Out of Zion, the perfection of beauty, God hath shined. Our God shall come, and shall not keep silence: a fire shall devour before him, and it shall be very tempestuous round about him. He shall call to the heavens from above, and to the earth, that he may judge his people. Gather my saints together unto me; those that have made a covenant with me by sacrifice. And the heavens shall declare his righteousness: for God is judge himself. Selah" (Psalms 50:1-6).

God is in the business of showing forth His beauty, perfecting the Saints with beauty, grace and glory. One of the ways He does it is through wealth and finances. He releases finances on His people. Get set for God's perfection. In as much as God wants to perfect beauty in Zion, the church; not everyone is entitled. Only those who have made a covenant with Him by sacrifice are entitled to this release. Zion is God's, but He is responsible for only those that are in covenant with Him through sacrifice. Do not leave your financial destiny to chance; establish it through covenant by sacrifice with the Lord.

When you are in a covenant by sacrifice with the Lord, your financial status in the kingdom is guaranteed.

- What is a covenant by sacrifice?

- What are the benefits?

- Examples of practitioners

- God demands it from you.

Understanding of these principles will establish your financial destiny.

What Is Covenant By Sacrifice?

Covenant: Is a legal agreement between two parties that

makes them responsible to one another; in the sense that they perform specific roles towards each other regardless of conditions. They are legally bound to each other.

Sacrifice: It is going the extra mile and beyond your convenience to make something happen for someone; stretching beyond your comfort levels to do something.

Joining the two terms, a covenant by sacrifice with God simply means you going the extra mile, away from your comfort zone, stretching beyond your limit, inconveniencing yourself to make something happen for God. When you sacrifice you are into covenant with the Lord.

Benefits of Covenant by Sacrifice

When you stretch beyond yourself, enduring the cost and inconveniences to make something happen for God, you are making God legally responsible for you, no matter what. If you go all the way to make something happen for God, He will go all the way to make something happen for you. God is bound by covenant.

There are many ways you can make a covenant by sacrifice with God for different needs.

- When you serve God sacrificially, He ensures you are cared for, healthy and alive.

- When you praise no matter what, He ensures your victory.

- When you give despise the cost, He blesses you abundantly; establishing your financial destiny.

What am I saying; sacrifice turns a promise into a covenant and commits God to perform His promises to you. Everyone is entitled to God's promises, but He is only responsible for those who have sacrificed and turned it into covenant. In your giving go extra mile to turn the promise of financial destiny into covenant; then you boldly say I have a covenant of financial destiny. That means regardless of you, your strength, the prevailing economic situation, God will establish your financial destiny. Covenant by sacrifice is direct line to having God's promises. I cannot live my financial destiny to chance, so I decided to make a covenant with Him by sacrifice.

One sacrifice is all you need per-time. Every redeemed person is God's, but all do not experience the same degree of provision. This is dependent on one's willingness to sacrifice.

Examples of Practitioners

Examples include Abraham, the Zarephath widow, the widow that gave her all, and Mary Magdalene.

God is always seeking people to enter into covenant with Him so that He can commit to them.

> *"For the eyes of the LORD run to and fro throughout the whole earth, to shew himself strong in the behalf*

of them whose heart is perfect toward him. Herein thou hast done foolishly: therefore from henceforth thou shalt have wars." (2 Chron. 16:9).

God is seeking those whose hearts are perfect towards him; those that love Him unconditionally and loves Him above everything else; and are willing to sacrifice.

Abraham

Abraham entered a covenant with the Lord by the circumcision of his flesh – what a sacrifice. (Gen.17:1-27, Gen. 22:1-19).

It is a covenant of fruitfulness and multiplication. This made God committed to blessing him despite his age. When God demanded Isaac, he willingly gave him up, and this made God eternally bound to his blessing. That's sacrifice for covenant.

The Zarephath Widow

The Zarephath widow gave her last meal to Elijah as commanded by God; that was a great sacrifice (1Kings 17).

What is God's commanding you to give? What do you have a strong nudge to give or do for the kingdom? That's God calling you into a covenant. It can never be the devil or self. The devil can never ask you to give to the kingdom of God nor would self-want you to. Please never give excuses to push it aside.

One day as I was thanking God for a cheque I had waited so long to receive, I had the desire and strong push to give it all to God. I did because I understood it was God commanding me. It could not have been I, because I needed it so much, it was God pushing me into covenant with Him. When I did, He told me He has established my Priesthood (ministry) forever. Though it was painful to me, the reward was great. Until it pains you, it is not yet a covenant.

Covenants are made with blood; that is a painful sacrifice of blood. That is why I can boldly say that God is committed to me in this ministry. It is a covenant. When the widow sacrificed; God established abundance for her and her household. God demanded a sacrifice because there was a need; His servant's welfare (Elijah) needed to be sustained.

The best time to covenant with God is when there is a need in the kingdom. Sacrifice for it and strike a covenant. There are opportunities to give to God sacrificially and enter a covenant with Him. Give your ears to God, let Him command you what to sacrifice.

I did not say give but sacrifice; the kind that you will give and crying. You cannot watch God's work die or remain at same level. You and I must sacrifice to take it to its next level. God is counting on us, not on the angels. I tell you we are able, and He can bless us as we give. That is why He demands a sacrifice.

David could not watch God's kingdom to suffer Psalms. (132:1-3). David was so passionate about God even at the risk of his life. He fought Goliath when everyone else hid. And these made God commit to him big time.

> *"My covenant will I not break, nor alter the thing that is gone out of my lips. Once have I sworn by my holiness that I will not lie unto David. His seed shall endure forever, and his throne as the sun before me. It shall be established forever as the moon, and as a faithful witness in heaven. Selah" (Psalms 89:34-37).*

Sacrifice is spiritual. It is not done with an unrenewed mindset. You have to renew your mind to that level, the level and attitude that makes it easy to sacrifice. This attitude enabled Abraham, the widow and the rest to sacrifice. (**Romans 4:17-22).**

This attitude makes you unstoppable by the pains of sacrifice. This is the attitude or mindset of being persuaded that God is all-powerful and can do all things. Believing He can make water come for you out of the rock. That even when you give all, and there is nothing left, that God is able to make something happen for you somehow.

Sacrificing what you depend on to depend on God. And

I tell you; God is able even if it means raising the dead for you. That was Abraham's thought when he sacrificed Isaac; that God was able to raise him (Isaac) up from dead.

God is able; it takes total trust in God to sacrifice, and that is when your faith is strong enough to receive your desire. Until your faith gets to the trust level, you will find it difficult to sacrifice. With trust, there is no alternative to God, and then He comes in quickly to help.

Sacrifice is saying "God I am giving up what you demanded, depending on you to fulfil your promises". Then you are free to thrive in His power and abundance. I have been in there several times, and He has never failed. When you are going through challenges; employ this secret, strike a covenant with the Lord by sacrifice and he will be committed to you.

There Have Been Testimonies To This

Solomon by sacrifice, received an open cheque; God told him to ask whatever he wanted. Do you desire an open cheque? Strike a covenant with God by sacrifice. Do not wait until there is a need in the kingdom; make sacrifice your way of life.

Challenges in your life present opportunities for sacrifice; when you sacrifice to God, He takes over and takes you out of the crisis. **(Genesis 28:10-22).**

When it looks like you are drowning, activate your lifebuoy by sacrifice. When you are in a situation that only God can save you, sacrifice what He demands and see Him step in and take you out of it.

> *"He that goeth forth and weepeth, bearing precious seed, shall doubtless come again with rejoicing, bringing his sheaves with him"* **(Psalms 126:6).**

When you sacrifice weeping, the harvest is guaranteed. There is no doubt about that.

Another opportunity to sacrifice is when you have had God's victory and deliverance; Noah made a covenant with God after he was delivered from the great flood. **(Genesis 8:20-22).** When God gives you an outstanding victory, deliverance, healing, etc., sacrifice something to establish it. Seize every opportunity, pay the price today and establish your great future by covenant. You have a great and glorious future, establish it by covenant.

> *"That I may perform the oath which I have sworn unto your fathers, to give them a land flowing with milk and honey, as it is this day. Then answered I, and said, So be it, O LORD"* **(Jer. 11:5).**

Provoke God by your sacrificial giving – the kind of giving you will be crying when giving and strike a covenant with him and He will be committed to you eternally. With covenant; you are good to go anywhere, knowing your back is covered.

God is mindful of His covenant with you once it is done. You might forget but He does not forget **(Psalms 105:8)** even to the thousand generations. You have limited power but God is limitless, He is all powerful; so get Him to work for you and be responsible for you through your sacrifice.

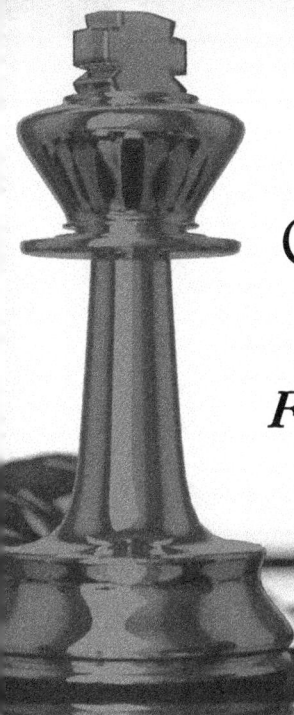

CHAPTER 9

Financial Harvest

For every seed you sow, surely there is a harvest. If nothing stopped you from sowing, nothing could stop your harvest. Your harvest is certain as day and night, summer and winter. There has never been a day without night. And there has been no year without summer and winter. This is how it is with sowing and reaping. Harvest (reaping) automatically follows sowing. For every seed both good and bad there is a harvest. If you need good harvest, begin to sow good seed. If you had in the past sown bad seed, you could ask God for mercy so that you will not reap evil. But you must repent and begin to sow the right seeds.

> *"While the earth remains, Seedtime and harvest,*
> *Cold and heat, Winter and summer, And day and night*
> *Shall not cease" (Genesis 8:22 NKJV).*

> *"Do not be deceived, God is not mocked; for whatever a man sows, that he will also reap" (Galatians 6:7 NKJV).*

> *"By the word of truth, by the power of God, by the armor of righteousness on the right hand and on the left" (2Cor 6:7 NKJV).*

> *"Give, and it will be given to you: good measure, pressed down, shaken together, and running over will be put into your bosom. For with the same measure that you use, it will be measured back to you" (Luke 6:38 NKJV).*

> *"He who continually goes forth weeping, bearing seed for sowing, shall doubtless come again with rejoicing, bringing his sheaves with him" (Psalms 126:6 NKJV).*

In this chapter, we are considering financial harvest. Teaching on financial destiny would not be complete without discussing how to harvest the financial seed you have sown. Harvesting financial seed is reaping the abundance of the seed you sowed. If you do not know how to harvest, your sowing would be a wasted effort. No doubt there is a harvest for every seed, but you must know how to harvest; otherwise, it will get spoiled, or thieves and the hungry will eat it up.

"Whose harvest the hungry eateth up, and taketh it even out of the thorns, and the robber swalloweth up their substance" *(Job 5:5).*

When God released manna, the Israelites gathered. Therefore you must know how to gather whatever God has released to you.

"That **thou givest them they gather: thou openest thine hand, they are filled with good"** *(Psalms 104:28).*

Christians have been taught so much on sowing, but little on how to harvest; this is why poverty prevails, and people are discouraged from giving. If both teachings are balanced, everyone will have a harvest of whatever he sows and increase, thereby making giving delightsome.

In this chapter, you shall learn to throw in your sickle for the harvest. You have sown, and your seeds have blossomed, it is your harvest now in the Mighty Name of Jesus. Knowledge is coming into you, and from today nothing shall hinder you from gathering your seeds.

There is time to scatter seeds, and there is time to gather. "A time to be born, And a time to die; A time to plant, And a time to pluck what is planted" (Eccl. 3:2 NKJV).

Now is your time to gather. Open your hearts to these principles, and you shall doubtlessly come in with sheaves rejoicing. There is a harvest for you that have been tithing, giving your offering, giving to your Pastors, investing in kingdom project etc. Your harvest is ready that is why God is bringing this word across to you.

How to Harvest

• Have An Expectation For Every Seed

Do not just cast your seed, have an expectation of harvest for every seed you sow even the least. No farmer goes about sowing seed without hope. Ask the farmer, and you will find out he has expectation for every seed he sows. The essence of sowing is harvest. "He that ploughs do it in hope". The reason we sow seed is simply to harvest.

Why then do people give without the expectation of harvest? They give their offering with nothing in mind, that's a wasted seed. If you must harvest; there should be an expectation. What is your expectation for giving that offering, tithe, prophet offering, etc.? There is no doubt that you give because you love God, but never give without expecting something in return from Him.

God is richer than you, so you are not giving to Him because He lacks, you are giving to receive from Him. There is a whole lot of difference giving to God and giving to men. You give to God to draw from His abundance. Your giving is to draw from Him, so be expectant.

Your giving is like a token for a release from Him, so expect it. Without expectation; the harvest will be right before you, but you will not see it. Many have missed their harvest because they were not expecting it.

> *"Cast your bread upon the waters, For you will find it after many days" (Eccl.11:1 NKJV).*

When you cast your bread, expect that after many days you will find it; so never give up on your expectation. Also, give in such a way that you will always remember what to expect from your seed. When you give casually (quantity and quality) you forget you did. No wonder David said I will not give God that which does not cost me anything.

> *"Then King David said to Ornan, "No, but I will surely buy it for the full price, for I will not take what is yours for the Lord, nor offer burnt offerings with that which costs me nothing" (1 Chro. 21:24 NKJV).*

Give something you will not forget too soon; give a costly seed. There are seeds you sow that you will never forget and as often as you remember them your expectation for your harvest is intact.

Until you sow in tears, you might not expect to come in with sheaves rejoicing

> *"He that goeth forth and weepeth, bearing precious seed, shall doubtless come again with rejoicing, bringing his sheaves with him" (Psalms 126:6).*

Another Question Should Be How Much To Expect?

Your expectation should not be the amount you sowed. Expect far more than that. When you give, you should expect press down, shaken together and running over kind of harvest. Expect as much as a farmer does from a grain of corn.

> *"Give, and it will be given to you: good measure, pressed down, shaken together, and running over will be put into your bosom. For with the same measure that you use, it will be measured back to you" (Luke 6:38 NKJV).*

Why Is It Necessary To Expect The Right Amount?

A wrong expectation is as good as no expectation. You do not get what you sowed but its multiplication. If it is same amount, then it is no harvest. If you expect same amount it will take forever to come because it is impossible.

God multiplies every seed you sow and gives it back to you. Therefore, begin to make accommodation for your abundant harvest. Budget for it before it arrives, that's faith at work that will bring the manifestation. There must be an expectation (hope) for faith to work.

> *"Now faith is the substance of things hoped for, the evidence of things not seen" (Heb.11:1).*

After expectation, the next necessary two steps are faith and patience. Be followers of them who through faith and patience, obtained the promise. There is a promise of abundant harvest, but you need faith and patience to obtain the promise.

Note: Your expectation is from God whom you have given and not from people or the church. Though you gave to people and the church, it is to God that you actually gave, and you should expect your harvest from Him. If God inspires your giving, it is Him that will reward you. Only Him is the Lord (owner) of the harvest.

There is nothing that frustrates faith than looking unto man or church for harvest. If your giving was God-inspired do not be discouraged nor offended, God will cause a release in due season. That means that after you have given, remove your eyes from the recipient and place your expectation on God. And I tell you, no one can meet your expectations like God.

Blessed is the man that does not look unto man for his harvest. Only the Lord is the God of harvest; no one is qualified to be the God of your harvest.

> *"So pray to the one in charge of the harvesting, and ask him to recruit more workers for his harvest fields" (Matt. 9:38 TLB).*

It is only from God you receive the reward of your seeds not from man. If you fix your eyes on man, you will miss your harvest. So never be offended when your church does not help you. They may be limited in resources, but God abounds in riches. Focus on God, not on men. I have heard stories of people that quit church because their church could not help them, that is not right.

Though you have been paying your tithe to the church, you were actually paying to God. If the church refuses to help, as long as you are not offended and your eyes are on God, help will surely come for you from God through other sources. But the problem is this; people get offended, leave the church, cut fellowship with God and thus miss their harvest.

Note: God is the rewarder of every tithe, offering, kingdom project, prophet offering, etc. not the church nor any man dead or alive. God is the rewarder of anything done in His name; let your motive be right. If not in the name of the Lord, do not give, or you will be disappointed.

Whenever you are giving to anyone or group, let it be in the name of the Lord, because it is God that rewards. If done outside His name, your reward is not guaranteed. Let your motive be right. Let the love of God be the reason you are giving, any other reason does not promise a harvest, regardless of whatever anyone tells you.

It is true that people give for different motives, and the true reflection of their motives is their reaction when harvest delays. When your harvest delays and you take offence in man or church, then your motivation is or was wrong. Repent and get your motivation right. Do not sow until your motive is right.

Do all things in the name of the Lord; stay put if the Lord did not send or inspire you. Keep your seed if your motive is other than God. This is the reason many seeds are wasted. When your purpose for giving is God, then you can have faith in Him for a bountiful harvest.

This Brings Us To The Next Step In Harvest.

• Faith

Faith is doing God's word. If your giving is preceded by God's word, then you have faith for your reward. The word that stirred you to give also ensures your harvest.

> *"My son, eat honey because it is good, And the honeycomb which is sweet to your taste; so shall the knowledge of wisdom be to your soul; If you have found it, there is a prospect, and your hope will not be cut off" (Proverbs 24:13–14 NKJV).*

Therefore search the word for your harvest. Every reward from God to you is via the vehicle of His word.

Peter obeyed the word of Jesus and found money in the mouth of a fish.

> *"Nevertheless, lest we offend them, go to the sea, cast in a hook, and take the fish that comes up first. And when you have opened its mouth, you will find a [a]piece of money; take that and give it to them for Me and you" (Matt. 17:27 NKJV).*

He heard the word, obeyed it and got a harvest. How on earth does it make sense to find money in the mouth of a fish? But Peter obeyed, and he did; this is faith. Your harvest might seem impossible, but the word created the world, only obey God's word to you and reap your harvest.

Do that which the Lord impresses on your heart to do. Invest in that business, attend that meeting, talk to that person, and whatever He tells you to do, please do it.

> *"And Simon answering said unto him, Master, we have toiled all the night, and have taken nothing: nevertheless at thy word I will let down the net" (Luke 5:5).*

Obey even if it does not make sense; that is faith. And I tell you; hardly does what God is asking you to do make sense. Your mind may attempt to resist it. Faith is simply doing what God tells you to do. When you do that, the power of God is released to cause a harvest for you. It might not be available now, but if you obey, power is released to create and make it happen for you. Though that money you expect to harvest is not available, if you obey what God is asking you to do, you will have it.

Peter obeyed when it made little or no sense, and he caught a multitude of fish. How many times have you turned down a nudge to do something? Unknowingly denying your harvest? Any word you refuse to obey denies your harvest. That offer to work a little extra time could be your harvest.

Faith, your uncompromising obedience to the word is your power for harvest.

> *"No man taketh it from me, but I lay it down of myself. I have power to lay it down, and I have power to take it again. This commandment have I received of my Father" (John 10:18).*

It is not enough to have the power to lay down your money when God commands, you should also have the power to take it up (harvest) by the same obedience to the commanded word. When you obey the commandment to sow, be careful to also obey the commandment (word) to harvest. If you care to obey the word to give, then be careful to obey the word and reap your harvest. Both commandants to give and harvest proceeds from the father (the God of harvest) be careful to obey both.

If God commanded you to give, wait on Him, He will surely give a commandment for your harvest.

Note: it is a commandment; that means it is not optional to obey if you desire a harvest. So do not let your mind get in the way of your harvest. Wait on God for His commandment. When you have sown, search the word and be sensitive to God for a word, and act on it and you will harvest. If you miss the word, you lose your harvest. If you are not busy to sow your money, then do not be too busy to sit waiting for the word for your harvest.

Do not be too busy for harvest. I tell you, the word of God is the field of sowing and reaping or harvesting. We sow by the word and reap by word. Everything you expect from God is delivered by His word. Therefore, one who sows and reaps must have ample time, and full allegiance to the word or harvest is not in view.

It is the word that guarantees your expectation. Though you are a giver, you may lack for lack of the word.

Sit down and develop the power to take up your harvest or your sowing will be meaningless. If you found time to work for the seeds you sow, then find time to read the word for the harvest. God is faithful by His word.

I can imagine many harvests that are wasted because people do not make time to study the word of God. One thing is to get the word, another thing is to obey. Once you find the word of your harvest, the next step is to obey it. Only in obeying; acting on the word, would your harvest be realized.

Many by natural wisdom (reasoning God's word) have denied their harvest. It was not human wisdom to give your money, therefore be foolish still to obey God's word and harvest. Do the unconventional that the Lord has commanded you.

> *"He that observeth the wind shall not sow; and he that regardeth the clouds shall not reap" (Ecclesiastic 11:4).*

If you observe the cloud, you will not reap. Another reason that stops believers from obeying God's word is **laziness.** If you must harvest, you must be diligent. How many times have you turned down the urge to write a proposal or enter a contest or submit a tender because of laziness and procrastination? "I am tired."

> *"He that gathereth in summer is a wise son: but he that sleepeth in harvest is a son that causeth shame" (Proverbs 10:5).*

> *"The desire of the slothful killeth him; for his hands refuse to labour" (Proverb 21:25).*

> *"The sluggard will not plow by reason of the cold; therefore shall he beg in harvest, and have nothing" (Proverbs 20:4).*

Most often, obeying God's word takes you away from your comfort zone. So be diligent in obeying. Put in that extra labour for your hundredfold harvest. When an opportunity to work an extra hour comes, seize it, and grace will be available to do it. For every labour, there is a profit. Your harvest might be that profit. Do not be lazy for God will make grace abound towards you for every good work.

> *"God is able to make it up to you by giving you everything you need and more so that there will not only be enough for your own needs but plenty left over to give joyfully to others" (2 Cor. 9:8 TLB).*

Every good work has the promise of a reward. God sometimes keeps your harvest as a reward for your service, so be diligent.

There is no food for the lazy man, even in the kingdom. Paul teaches that he that does not work should not eat.

> *"Even while we were still there with you, we gave you this rule: "He who does not work shall not eat" (2 Thess. 3:10 TLB).*

If you are diligent to sow, then be diligent in harvesting.

> *"Slothfulness casts into deep sleep" (Prov. 19:15).*

So wake up and harvest. Invest your time doing something useful. As a child, do chores for your parents, aunties, uncles, etc. God might have kept the harvest of your giving as a reward for these services.

Volunteer to help, it might be your harvest. Do not watch opportunities slip by, rise up and seize them. These are likely reasons people miss their harvest and blame God. If you are not lazy to seek and obey the word, you will find out that financial prosperity message works.

Laziness and disobedience to the word are reasons people are not prospered and why they criticise prosperity messages. It is God's will for you to give and reap a harvest for your financial increase, but you must follow His ways.

Prosperity message works, if it does not work for you, probably you have refused to work it for your benefit.

• Patience

No matter how good seed is, no farmer sows today and reaps immediately. Time is needed for every harvest. You do not plant today and reaps the next day. As sure as the harvest is, time is required, so be patient. If you wait for that which is sure you have to be patient.

After you have sown be patient, keep sowing and watering your seeds. (**Galatians 6:9, Heb.10:36, Heb.6:12-20, Eccl.11:1-6).**

After casting your seed, it takes many days for the harvest to come. You need to have patience after you have done the work of sowing to obtain the harvest. Impatience and anxiety destroy your seeds.

Some harvests are sooner than others, just like all seed do not need equal time to grow and mature. As you sow, your cloud is getting filled with water and when it is saturated it rains and delivers your blessings. For the harvest, you need patient endurance to keep sowing. Do not stop filling your cloud with your seed for it will definitely rain. I can hear the sound of abundant rain for you. I call forth your incredible harvest in Jesus' Mighty Name. You are the next in line for a testimony.

You shall not faint. May God's strength abound for your harvest? Do not give up, your harvest is closer than you thought, your field is ripe for harvest. Run to Jezreel (the word, the field) for I can see the rain coming. **(1Kings 18:41-46).** If only you will be patient enough to wait and look the seventh time, you will surely not miss it.

• Righteousness

If you desire to harvest, sowing does not authorize you to live unholy. The fact that you give your money to God is not a license nor bribe to break His word and live like you please. **(Jeremiah 5:24, Jeremiah 4:3-4, Hosea 10:12-13).**

Sin makes you sow on fallow ground; amongst thorns without hope of harvest. A wise farmer cultivates the land and gets rid of weeds the thorns before sowing. Otherwise, the thorns will choke the seed and prevent it from producing a harvest. Do not think that you can bribe God with your money and continuing in sin; that's impossible.

God is not interested in your money if you do not allow His word to change you by breaking that pride, arrogance, and disobedience to authority, fornication, adultery, and every kind of immorality.

If you will not allow the word of God change you, keep your money. God is more interested in your soul than your money. Sin blocks your harvest. Sin constitutes a barrier to your harvest.

> *"Look, the Lord's hand is not too weak to deliver you; his ear is not too deaf to hear you. But your sinful acts have alienated you from your God; your sins have caused him to reject you and not listen to your prayers" (Isaiah 59:1-2 NET).*

You cannot harvest in unrighteousness. No wonder Jesus said if you come to the altar to give and you remember your brother has a case against, leave your offering and go and settle with your brother and come back and give your offering; otherwise it is futile.

> *"So then, if you bring your gift to the altar and there remember that your brother has something against you, leave your gift there in front of the altar. First go and be reconciled to your brother and then come and present your gift" (Matt. 5:23-24 NET).*

Jeremiah says it is another way "break up your fallow ground and sow not amongst thorns." Every stone and thorns in your heart constitute a hindrance to your harvest. Pride, bitterness, strife, envy etc. Constitute these stones and thorns, and until you rid them from your heart, your harvest does not count. They must go before your seed attracts a harvest. **(Read Jeremiah 4:3-4, Hosea 10:12-13).**

Sin does not go with the harvest. Sin is anti-harvest, like the little foxes that destroy the vine.

> *"Catch us the foxes, the little foxes that spoil the vines, For our vines have tender grapes" (Song of Solomon 2:15 NKJV).*

Sin eats up harvest. Nothing makes a land sick than sin. God's grace abounds for He has promised to heal our land.

- Ask

> *"Give, and it shall be given unto you; good measure, pressed down, and shaken together, and running over, shall men give into your bosom. For with the same measure that ye mete withal it shall be measured to you again" (Luke 6:38).*

When you give, God will cause men to give unto your bosom. It is true that your harvest is from God, but He supplies through man. After you asked God for harvest, He moves men to give you. But sometimes He might direct you to ask them. Then when you ask as God commanded, it shall be given unto you.

When God instructs you to ask someone, He must have put your harvest in his hand and will stir the person's heart to give it to you. Asking is different from begging, you ask as commanded by God, but begging is self-originated, trial and luck business. With asking you do not miss your harvest. Someone seating next to you might have your reward, but how will you know if you do not ask, and how will you ask if not commanded? Therefore be sensitive to God to know who to ask.

Do not be too proud to ask, or you miss your harvest. Elijah asked the Zarephath widow. Jesus' disciples asked the lad for his five loaves and two fishes. They also asked for the room set for the Passover meal. That neighbour may have information you need for that job you have been praying for; open your mouth and ask. Ask, and it shall be given to you.

> *"Ask, and it shall be given you; seek, and ye shall find; knock, and it shall be opened unto you: For every one that asketh receiveth; and he that seeketh findeth, and to him that knocketh it shall be opened" (Matt. 7:7-8).*

Asking is heavenly instruction to the specific person God has kept your reward with. You cannot ask everyone, but you can beg everyone. Then it is no longer asking, it has become begging and you have turned to a beggar. Begging is anti-kingdom.

Remember it is your right to reap because you have sown, so do not be beggarly in your asking. I had sown my resources into our publication ministry, after the thirtieth book, God commanded me to ask someone to invest in it, I did, and the Lord honoured His word.

I heard a testimony of a couple that has been sowing into the kingdom. When the wife needed money about $35,000 for her training, God instructed them to ask a particular couple, when they did, there was no hesitation because the Lord had already told that couple. This lady got her money freely, not as a loan. It was given to her not to pay back. This is because it was her harvest from God. His blessing (reward) makes rich and adds no sorrow.

> *"The blessing from the Lord makes a person rich, and he adds no sorrow to it" (Prov. 10:22 NET).*

You may not have it in your account right now, it is somewhere in someone's possession or custody, and at the due time, God will direct you to ask the right person. Keep sowing and be diligent in your business. I command your ears and eyes to be open to see the person with your reward.

No More Begging

Begging is not permitted in the kingdom, but God can lead you to ask. God only leads sowers to ask. Those that did not sow end up begging and are ridiculed. When you ask, it will be pleasurable to the person to give you because he had been touched by God. Money circulates, so your financial harvest might be in the hand of someone; let God lead you to ask and move it to you.

Note: you must first ask God then He may direct you to whom to ask or cause people to supply you without your asking. God is not bound to a particular way.

It is God's business to reward you, follow Him and never assume a specific way.

> *"But this I say: He who sows sparingly will also reap sparingly, and he who sows bountifully will also reap bountifully. So let each one give as he purposes in his heart, not grudgingly or of necessity; for God loves a cheerful giver. And God is able to make all grace abound toward you, that you, always having all sufficiency in all things, may have an abundance for every good work. As it is written: "He has dispersed abroad, He has given to the poor; His righteousness endures forever." Now may He who supplies seed to the sower, and bread for food, [e]supply and multiply the seed you have sown and increase the fruits of your righteousness, while you are enriched in everything for all liberality, which causes thanksgiving through us to God" (2Cor. 9:6-11).*

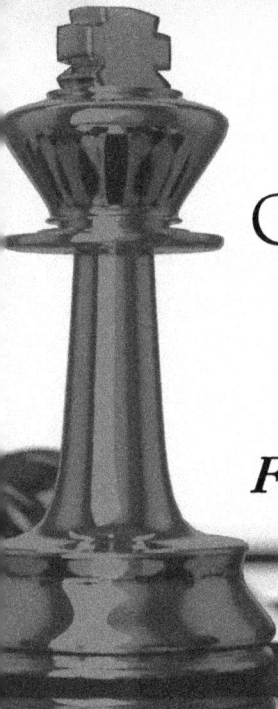

CHAPTER 10

Facilitators of Financial Harvest

In the previous chapter, it was established that harvest follows every seed sown, though it is not immediate. There is a time lag between sowing and harvesting. In this chapter, I will show you what could facilitate your harvest. What you can do to make your harvest sooner than usual. Just like in the natural there are things that make seeds grow faster and produce a harvest earlier. In the context of this topic I call them facilitators of financial harvest; things that make your financial harvest quicker and more than you thought.

Mercy

> *"Sow to yourselves in righteousness, reap in mercy; break up your fallow ground: for it is time to seek the LORD, till he come and rain righteousness upon you" (Hosea 10:12).*

It takes mercy to harvest your financial seeds and every other seed. Mercy is what singles you out and makes it your turn for harvest. It is mercy that proffers protection on your seeds and keeps them safe for harvest.

What is Mercy?

God's mercy is defined as the loving kindness of God; His tender kindness that picks you out for favour. (Romans 9:10-21, Luke 4:25-27, Luke 5:3, John 5:5-6).

Mercy is the principal factor in harvest. He that sows and waters are insignificant to harvest for it is God that gives life. It is not of him that willeth, nor runneth, but God that shows mercy. No wonder it was recorded that Isaac sowed and received a hundredfold for the Lord blessed him.

> *"12 Then Isaac sowed in that land, and received in the same year an hundredfold: and the Lord blessed him"(Gen. 26:12).*

He did not earn hundredfold but received it. Received indicates it was given to him. It was given to him from above (God).

"John answered and said, A man can receive nothing, except it be given him from heaven" (John 3:27).

Permit me to say that your financial harvest is a receivable, not an achievement. Everything you have in this kingdom is a gift to you. Never could you have worked for it. It is a gift from above.

Tell me what you could pay or work to earn salvation, you do not deserve it but given to you. Salvation is a free gift by grace, so is every other thing that follows.

"He that spared not his own Son, but delivered him up for us all, how shall he not with him also freely give us all things" (Romans 8:32).

Sowing or giving puts you on the line for harvest, but mercy spots you out and makes it your turn. (Ecclesiastics 9:11. Psalms 33:16-22).

You are not qualified for harvest by your works of sowing because no amount could qualify for the kind of harvest Gods gives. You sow one grain and harvest sheaves – that is mercy.

Nothing you will ever give matches the harvest God gives. More so the seed you sowed was given to you by God. (Isaiah 55:10b, I Corinthians 9:10, Romans 11:35-36). Even the willingness to sow was from God.

"For it is God which worketh in you both to will and to do of his good pleasure" (Philippians 2:13).

It is so evident that nothing is yours in these stages of sowing and reaping. (Romans 11:36). Understanding the role of mercy is very important to have the right attitude for the harvest. Your harvest is not a right but a privilege. Until you develop the right attitude you will miss your harvest. Reap in mercy that is; develop an attitude to attract God's mercy. (Luke 18:10-14).

Never have the attitude that you are taking back from God what you sowed or an attitude that God owes you. God cannot owe anyone because all things are His. God does not owe anyone, even you, no matter what you sowed. Also if you sold yourself and gave the money, after all He made and owns you and you are giving Him back what is His. Everything is God's. Cattles upon a thousand hills are God's. (Haggai 2:8, Psalms 24:1-2).

God is not a money doubler; He is your father that wants to bless you financially out of His rich abundance. Therefore approach Him on the platform of mercy. Everything is His, so only mercy makes Him give it to you. Your attitude should be *"Lord, I do not deserve that much harvest but let your mercy prevail and make it mine."* Everything God gives is on the platform of mercy not as a reward, pay, nor right. Financial harvest is an act of God's mercy, and yours is the next on line. If you are approaching financial harvest based on the much you have sown, you will be disappointed. What is it you have and sowed that you did not receive? If you received why do you behave as though you did not receive it?

If financial harvest is on the platform of mercy why then do I need to sow? (Romans 6:1, Micah 6:8, Hosea 10:12). Your sowing is expression of your love and obedience to God; walking in humility which puts you in the list of those to obtain mercy. Disobedience to the word of God, e.g. as regards giving, puts you far away to be considered. Noah obtained mercy because he was righteous before God; he did all that God commanded. The Lord resists the proud but shows grace to the humble.

> *"Surely he scorneth the scorners: but he giveth grace unto the lowly" (Prov. 3:34).*

Moreover, your seed is a token God works on for your harvest. When you have sown and are picked by mercy; then God releases a word for your harvest, telling you what to do to harvest or where to find your harvest.

The word also gives you expectation, enables you to walk righteously and be patient. These constitute the power to take up. Mercy gives you the ability to take up and make that power effective. If mercy is this important for harvest, then you must know how to obtain mercy.

How To Obtain Mercy

• Give Your Life To Jesus

"Which in time past were not a people, but are now the people of God: which had not obtained mercy, but now have obtained mercy" (1Peter 2:10).

God's mercy is packaged in Jesus. When you receive Jesus, you receive God's mercy. You cannot refuse God's mercy in the gifts of His son and have it some other way. All the goodness of God is on the platform of salvation by Christ Jesus.

• Have The Attitude Of Thanksgiving

Give thanks to God for everything you received. Be grateful for the least and great. Cease to complain. Those that complained and murmured in the wilderness over God's provision were destroyed. After sowing and the harvest seem to delay or not as much as you expected; be thankful to God. (2 Cor. 4:1, Psalm 130:5-8, Joel 2:23-27).

• *Ask For Mercy*

God is merciful and diligent in showing mercy so ask Him. (Hebrews 4:16, Psalms 67:1, Psalms 130:4-8).

- *Show Mercy To Others*

Be tender-hearted to one another. Show mercy to others, and you are sowing to reap it into your life. Do something for someone freely even if he does not deserve it. Pray for those that despitefully use you. Give someone more than he deserves; do not pay evil for evil. When you do these; you are sowing to reap in due season. He that shows mercy does good to his own soul.

> *"The merciful man doeth good to his own soul: but he that is cruel troubleth his own flesh" (Proverbs 11:17).*

When you show mercy; you are positioning yourself for God's mercy.

> *"Blessed are the merciful: for they shall obtain mercy" (Matt. 5:7).*

Children show mercy to your parents. Parents show mercy to your children. Husbands show your wife more kindness than she deserves, and wives do the same, and you shall reap the mercy of God. Refusal to show mercy can disqualify you from your financial harvest.

> *"The horse is **prepared against the day of battle:** but safety is of the LORD" (Proverbs 21:13).*

Remember the story of the servant the master forgave, but who refuses to forgive the fellow servant, and what his master did to him. Do not allow trend and society to prevent you from showing mercy to others or your life will be void of mercy. It is the trend to mind your own business in today's world; this is anti-scripture. The Bible says to bear one another's burden.

From now onwards, God's mercy shall prevail in your life. God will pick you for harvest. God will show you mercy and cause men to favour you for your harvest. Today; I declare rain of His mercy on every seed you have sown in His kingdom for harvest. The set time to favour you has come; it is now. Thrive in your financial harvest and increase. Expect the impossibility this week and send me your testimony. Where you have failed, God's mercy shall prevail. I call forth that miracle you desire; it is yours in Jesus' name.

God is set to release that miracle job into your hands; it is done by mercy.

Halleluyah.

CHAPTER 11

Instruments of Financial Harvest

In this chapter, we shall be considering the instrument of financial harvest. That is; the person God uses to bring to pass your financial harvest. This is the major means of your financial harvest.

"Have faith in the LORD your God, and you will be upheld; have faith in his prophets, and you will be successful" (2 Chronicle 20:20b).

Please read that in different bible versions; King James, Amplified, NAS, NIV, Good News, Living Version etc.

Concerning your prosperity, which financial harvest is a significant part of, God's prophets and servants play a cardinal role.

Who Are God's Prophets?

They are human messengers by whom God reveals His word and will to you. Today prophets unfold God's will as contained in His word. God's words they make known to you determines your harvest. The word they preach creates and enables your harvest.

Therefore, if you must believe the word they preach and teach to the same degree, you believe God if it were God speaking to you. Of course, you should because what they speak is word from God.

> *"How then shall they call on him in whom they have not believed? And how shall they believe in him of whom they have not heard? And how shall they hear without a preacher? And how shall they preach, except they are sent? As it is written, How beautiful are the feet of them that preach the gospel of peace, and bring glad tidings of good things" (Rom. 10:14-15).*

You cannot believe God more than His will, He has revealed to you in His word. How much you believe God is determined by your belief (acceptance and obedience) to His word He has revealed through His servants (preached word).

This is the primary reason many do not prosper, they believe in God, but they do not obey the word preached with the same intensity as though God would speak some other way than His word.

> *"For we have heard the Good News, just as they did. They heard the message, but it did them no good because when they heard it, they did not accept it with faith" (Hebrew 4:2 GNT).*

How much you believe and do the word of God that is preached to you per time determines the extent you prosper in the kingdom. This is a simple truth you must accept. Every word of God to you is intended to prosper you, so accept and obey it.

> *"And now, brethren, I commend you to God, and to the word of his grace, which is able to build you up, and to give you an inheritance among all them which are sanctified" (Acts 20:32).*

You are not doing the prophet favour by believing the word; you are doing it for yourself. More so, you do not believe it for the sake of the prophet, you believe simply because it is the word that is preached.

> *"Who confirms the word of His servant, And performs the counsel of His messengers; Who says to Jerusalem, 'You shall be inhabited,' To the cities of Judah, 'You shall be built,' And I will raise up her waste places" (Isaiah 44:26 NKJV).*

If you receive a prophet in the name of God (accept and obey the word he preaches), you will receive the prophet's reward. Prophet's reward is God confirming His word in your life.

So if you desire financial harvest this season, you must believe and obey what I have conveyed to you through this book. You must abide by it as though God was physically speaking to you; because I am a messenger sent by God to establish your financial harvest. If you do not obey, you will miss out of your harvest.

> *"Thou leddest thy people like a flock by the hand of Moses and Aaron" (Psalms 77:20).*

God's servants are great tools in God's hands to establish your destiny, even your financial destiny. God promised the Israelites the land, and Joshua gave it to them. You cannot ignore the word spoken to you by God's messenger and be established in your financial destiny.

How To Believe The Prophet

Believe what he says as you would if God was physically speaking to you. For no prophet speaks on his own, but inspired by God. Accept it wholeheartedly and unreservedly, committing your life to it and watch God honor his words (Acts 17:11, Acts 16:14).

- Act On It

If there is an action to take, do it. Do your part of the word, and God will do His part. Believing the prophet is doing good warfare with the word spoken to you, war with it in obedience until it comes to pass. God watches over His word to perform.

- Write It Down

You might forget if you do not write it down. The word charts your great destiny.

Why Do I Need To Believe The Prophet?

He is God's oracles and messenger to you. He teaches and preaches the word and will of God to you. And until you believe it will not come to pass.

> *"Who has believed our report? And to whom has the arm of the LORD BEEN REVEALED? (Isaiah 53:1 NKJV).*

> *"But we speak the wisdom of God in a mystery, the hidden wisdom which God ordained before the ages for our glory" (1 Cor. 2:7 NKJV).*

When you believe and obey, it releases glory on you. The prophet preaches not to make you happy and entertained, he preaches because God has given him a message for you. So take it seriously.

> *"And blessed is she that believed: for there shall be a performance of those things which were told her from the Lord" (Luke 1:45).*

The widow of Zarephath entered into her great financial destiny simply by obeying Elijah, also did the prophet's widow by obeying Elisha. They both obeyed what was said to them and obtained financial harvest. They obeyed immediately. When you delay to obey, you might lose the grace to obey because as you ponder and delay, it may no longer make sense to obey.

Every word carries grace that makes it seasonal. It is your season of financial harvest because this word carries grace that will enable you to do and obtain. When you miss this season, you lose your harvest. Cash in on any season God has brought by the word because fruits are readily available at their seasons. This is how God moves His people from phase to phase, even you.

I assure you that if you obey the word of God, the word the prophet preaches, you will be established and prosper. You are in the kingdom that makes men prosperous even financially, only let off your breaks; obey God sheepishly so that you can lie down in a green pasture.

> *"You led Your people like a flock By the hand of Moses and Aaron" (Psalms 77:20).*

For you that are reading this book, prosperity will no longer be a struggle; you will lie in it. That is; you will make money without struggles. Only let God lead you like a sheep by the hand of His prophet that He has placed in your life. He will guide you by the integrity and sincerity of his heart.

If God did not trust His Prophet, He will not make Him one nor commit your precious soul to him to lead and guide. If God trusts him with your soul, you can trust him with your money; doing what he asks you to do. I tell you if you follow his teaching of the word you will prosper. Many have been established in their financial destiny by committing to their Pastors. You are the next in line to be established.

You may not see where God is taking you, but you can believe the word that is preached and get there. Many have arrived at their financial destinies through my teachings.

> *"This book of the law shall not depart out of thy mouth; but thou shalt meditate therein day and night, that thou mayest observe to do according to all that is written therein: for then thou shalt make thy way prosperous, and then thou shalt have good success" (Joshua 1:8).*

The preached word charts the course of your financial destiny. God has a significant financial future for you, and if the prophet dilutes the word to suit you, he will be surcharging your great destiny. Do not think God's servants enjoy asking you to give or want to see you suffer but that's the only way you can be blessed. I am sure if there were other ways, we would gladly preach it because no one loves to be seen as a beggar or gold digger or be tagged all sorts of names. If we teach it, is for your good so that you will be blessed.

> *"For I have not shunned to declare unto you all the counsel of God" (Acts 20:27).*

If your pastor is a man of integrity and there is financial transparency in his dealings and using of God's money for what is said, then do not see him as a gold digger to rip off your money or you will miss out on what God is doing and miss your prosperity.

When you are asked to give above the ordinary, it is for your glorious destiny. To whom much is given, much is expected. When you are shown a picture of your destiny, a course is been charted, follow it even when it seems there is nothing to affirm it. I tell you, you will arrive there. God can raise a beggar from a dunghill to dine with princes. He needs nothing to do this rather than fulfilling His word that His prophet has spoken over your life.

Identify your contact point of blessing, believe in him or her. Do not allow familiarity to make you lose focus. Jesus could not do much in His town because of familiarity, the attitude of the people.

Above every other thing that you might consider your

pastor to be, He is sent by God to enable you to realise your destiny by the word. His role in your financial destiny is like that of a shepherd that sees green pasture and leads the sheep to it. The journey may be demanding and tasking, but love for the sheep would not let him stop urging. He may know the plights of the sheep but still encourages them to keep going so that they will be fed and experience no more lack.

God expects you to believe His messengers and He is displeased when you do not.

> *"Then he said unto them, O fools, and slow of heart to believe all that the prophets have spoken" (Luke 24:25).*

There is no alternative; nothing changes if you do not obey the word preached. There is nothing God can do for you outside His word. His words are what He uses to create and do things.

When the rich man in hell asked Abraham to send someone from the dead to warn his brother, Abraham replied, they have prophets, if they do not believe them, they would not believe even if someone rises from the dead.

No wonder the disciples asked,

> *"Lord, to whom shall we go? Thou hast the words of eternal life."(John 6:68).*

I do not think you are left with a choice if you do not obey the preached word of God. Jesus pointed out reasons people do not believe the revealed word; foolishness, dullness, sluggishness of heart, etc.

Remove every foolishness, dullness and sluggishness of the heart. Until these are gotten rid of, you will find it difficult to believe the preached word.

I pray that God will cause His Spirit to rest upon you to quicken your understanding, that your eyes will be enlightened by His will and purpose, and then you will find it delightsome to believe His prophets for your good.

May the Lord make you quick to understand spiritual things. I break every veil of covering over your minds. You need a prophet; God's messenger to take you to your destiny by the word – **Believe him**.

Your financial comfort is very close. It's been night seasons of sowing, sacrifice and weeping but I tell you, your harvest is sooner than you think. Do not give up hope though you may not see it, it is right nigh. Just follow the preached word, and you will reap.

I announce to you like Elijah did to Ahab; it is a new day for you. I can hear the sound of abundance of rain and miracles. Stress is over. God is opening new doors for you in Jesus name; Amen!

It is your morning of harvest; you are coming in with your sheaves rejoicing. It is your day; it is your glorious season.

www.ingramcontent.com/pod-product-compliance
Lightning Source LLC
Chambersburg PA
CBHW032035040426
42449CB00007B/900